Stefan Świeżawski

St. Thomas Revisited

Translated by Theresa Sandok, OSM

PETER LANG

New York • Washington, D.C./Baltimore • San Francisco
Bern • Frankfurt am Main • Berlin • Vienna • Paris

B
765
.T54
S8513
1995

Library of Congress Cataloging-in-Publication Data

Swieżawski, Stefan.
    [Swiety Tomasz na nowo odczytany. English]
    St. Thomas revisited / Stefan Władysław Swieżawski; translated by Theresa
Sandok.
        p.   cm. — Catholic thought from Lublin; 8)
    Includes bibliographical references.
    1. Thomas, Aquinas, Saint, 1225?–1274 I. Title. II. Series.
    B765.T54S8513   189'.4—dc20   94-16094
    ISBN 0-8204-1844-7
    ISSN 1051-693X

Die Deutsche Bibliothek-CIP-Einheitsaufnahme

Swieżawski, Stefan Władysław:
St. Thomas revisited / Stefan Władysław Swieżawski. Transl. by Theresa
Sandok. - New York; Washington D.C./Baltimore; San Francisco; Bern;
Frankfurt am Main; Berlin; Vienna; Paris: Lang
    (Catholic thought from Lublin; Vol. 8)
    ISBN 0-8204-1844-7
NE: GT

The paper in this book meets the guidelines for permanence and durability of
the Committee on Production Guidelines for Book Longevity of the
Council on Library Resources.

To my best friend
and companion
"on the way"—
my dearest Mary,

I dedicate this work.

St. Thomas Revisited

Catholic Thought from Lublin

Andrew Woznicki
General Editor

Vol. 8

PETER LANG
New York • Washington, D.C./Baltimore • San Francisco
Bern • Frankfurt am Main • Berlin • Vienna • Paris

Contents

Translator's Preface

Stefan Swiezawski (pronounced shfyeh-*jäf*-skee) was born in Holubie, Poland, on February 10, 1907. He studied philosophy and history at the University of Lwów, from which he received his doctorate in 1932. After teaching for a time at the Jagiellonian University in Krakow, Swiezawski joined the faculty of the Catholic University of Lublin, where he served for thirty years (1946–1976) as professor of philosophy and director of the division of the history of philosophy.

World War II and its aftermath took a heavy toll on the faculty of the Catholic University of Lublin, leaving the ranks of the philosophy department all but decimated. Together with Jerzy Kalinowski, Swiezawski set about building up the philosophy department by recruiting the best and brightest young Catholic minds in the country: Mieczyslaw A. Krapiec, Karol Wojtyla, Stanislaw Kaminski, and Marian Kurdzialek. Each of these six scholars, working together in close collaboration, concentrated on developing particular areas of philosophy—Krapiec on metaphysics and epistemology, Wojtyla on ethics and philosophical anthropology, Kaminski on methodology and philosophy of science, Kurdzialek and Swiezawski on the history of philosophy, and Kalinowski on logic and the philosophy of law—giving birth to what is known today as the Lublin School of Philosophy.

In 1929, while in Paris working on his doctoral thesis on Duns Scotus, Swiezawski met Étienne Gilson and attended some of his seminars. This encounter blossomed into a lifelong friendship that had important ramifications for Swiezawski's own philosophical development as well as for the future of the Lublin School of Philosophy. In 1934, Gilson published part of Swiezawski's doctoral thesis in French in the *Archives d'histoire doctrinale et littéraire du moyen âge*. Many years later, in 1956, Gilson invited Stefan Swiezawski and his wife Mary to Poitiers for a week-long visit. The communist authorities in Poland were reluctant to let the Swiezawskis out of the country, but through the intercession of the distinguished Marxist philosopher Adam Schaff the Swiezawskis obtained passports and set off for their first trip abroad since the war.

Stefan Swiezawski brought with him to France a compendium of works by philosophers from the Catholic University of Lublin to show to Gilson. Gilson was deeply impressed with the breadth and quality of the philosophical activity that had been going on at the Catholic University of Lublin during the oppressive Stalinist era and helped publicize the accomplishments of the Lublin philosophers. He later invited Swiezawski to return to France in 1960–61 and again in 1964–65 as *maître de recherche* at the *Centre National de la Recherche Scientifique* in Paris.

During the Second Vatican Council, Swiezawski participated in the deliberations as a lay auditor, a distinction no doubt attributable to the esteem in which he was held by his friend and colleague at the Catholic University of Lublin, Archbishop Karol Wojtyla. In 1989 Swiezawski was awarded an honorary doctorate by the Jagiellonian University in Krakow.

Swiezawski is the author of some thirty books and numerous articles in Polish, French, and German. His principal works in Polish include *Being* (Lublin: Catholic University of Lublin, 1948), *A Treatise on the Human Being* (Poznan: Pallottinum, 1956), *The Problem of the History of Philosophy* (Warsaw: Panstwowe Wydawnictwo Naukowe, 1966), and an eight-volume study of late medieval philosophy entitled *The History of European Philosophy in the 15th Century* (Warsaw/Krakow 1974–1990). This last work was abridged and edited by M. Prokopowicz and published in a one-volume French edition entitled *Histoire de la philosophie européenne au XVème siècle* (Paris: Beauchesne, 1990). With Jerzy Kalinowski, Swiezawski co-authored a book on Vatican II entitled *La philosophie à l'heure du Concile* (Paris: Société d'éditions internationales, 1965). A number of Swiezawski's more important philosophical essays have been collected into three anthologies and published in Polish as *Reason and Mystery* (1960), *The Human Being and Mystery* (1978), and *Existence and Mystery* (1993).

The present work originally appeared in Polish in 1983 and was subsequently translated into French by Marie Stokowska and Éric Ibarra, and published under the title *Redécouvrir Thomas d'Aquin* (Paris: Nouvelle cité, 1989).

A few words are in order here concerning the birthplace of *St. Thomas Revisited*. This book grew out of a lecture series presented by Stefan Swiezawski at Laski, an internationally renowned educational center for the visually impaired located near Warsaw and owned and operated by the

Society for the Care of the Blind. Both the center and the Society owe their origin to the visionary inspiration of Rose Czacka, a wealthy, well-educated Polish countess born in the Ukraine in 1876, who lost her sight at the age of twenty-two.

Czacka accepted her blindness as both a cross and a gift from God and took it as a sign that she was to devote her life to the service of the blind. She prepared herself for this task by traveling abroad to visit various institutions for the rehabilitation of the blind, by schooling herself in the science of the causes and treatment of blindness, and by mastering Braille. In 1911, she founded the Society for the Care of the Blind and gathered around her a group of volunteers to transcribe books into Braille. That same year, she established a kindergarten, a boarding school for boys, and a retirement home for women in Warsaw.

In 1917, Czacka entered a Franciscan novitiate in eastern Poland, where she received her initial formation in religious life and took the name Sister Elizabeth. She returned to Warsaw a year later to continue her work with the Society and to found the Congregation of Franciscan Sisters, Servants of the Cross, a religious community dedicated to the care of the visually impaired. Later that year the Society received a gift of twelve acres of land in Laski. The Society built a home for twenty-five children on the property and in 1922 moved its headquarters to Laski.

The period between the wars was a time of dramatic expansion at Laski, both in the physical and in the cultural sense. By 1938, the complex had grown to eleven buildings, including dormitories, schools, shops, a library, a retreat house, a chapel, and a hospital, and occupied over 125 acres of land. At the same time, Laski was developing into a dynamic center for intellectual and cultural exchange, attracting scientists from various fields and intellectuals from diverse political and religious persuasions, thanks to the spirit of freedom, openness, and ecumenism that prevailed there.

All of this came to a devastating halt at the outbreak of World War II. Because of its proximity to Warsaw, Laski became one of the first victims of the German invasion of Poland in September 1939. Four days of heavy bombing left seventy percent of its buildings in ruins. Mother Elizabeth herself was seriously wounded during the siege. In 1944, the Society for the Care of the Blind joined in the Warsaw uprising and operated field hospitals for the Home Army. Immediately after the war, Mother Elizabeth and her associates started rebuilding the complex with donations from at home and abroad, tripling its size and adding a school for mentally handicapped blind children, the only facility of its kind in Poland.

Over the years, thousands of visually impaired children have been nurtured and educated at Laski in the spirit of Mother Elizabeth's approach to the blind, which aims at integrating them into the fullness of human affairs and educating them to be responsible, contributing members of society. Laski also continues to be a refuge for those seeking spiritual enlightenment. In the words of former prime minister Tadeusz Mazowiecki, himself a frequent visitor to the center, Laski is a place where "the sighted can see more clearly."

THERESA H. SANDOK, OSM

Bellarmine College
Louisville, Kentucky
November 1993

Note to the English Edition

I am deeply grateful to Sister Theresa Sandok, OSM, for undertaking and carrying out the difficult work of translating this book into English. I hope that, as a result of her very clear and accurate translation, this book will help English-speaking readers better understand the philosophical thought of St. Thomas. I also wish to thank the publisher Peter Lang for making possible the publication of this book, which is the first of my works to appear in English. This all came about thanks to the kindness and initiative of the editor of the Catholic Thought from Lublin series, Rev. Prof. Andrew Woznicki, to whom I wish to express my special gratitude.

STEFAN SWIEZAWSKI

Warsaw
July 1993

Foreword

The book I place before you has—like every other book—a history of its own. It evolved in three stages. First there was an extended period of about fifty years. In that half-century segment of my life, I had the opportunity repeatedly and in various ways to encounter the thought of St. Thomas Aquinas. This encounter took the form of a more or less systematic reading of his works. It also entailed a study of the literature on his writings, particularly the more recent literature. Finally, it involved lecturing on his views, and specifically on his philosophy. I presented these lectures both in university settings, as regular and monographic courses in the history of philosophy, and also in abbreviated form, as series designed to acquaint various groups with Thomas' thought. In this way, over the course of many years, the basic structure of the subject matter presented in the twenty-five chapters of this book gradually developed. The material accumulated in this way, however, would never have seen the printed page were it not for the second stage of the book's history.

This second stage began in 1977, when Sister Alma Skrzydlewska, Superior General of the Congregation of the Franciscan Sisters, Servants of the Cross, approached me with the proposal of presenting a series of lectures to the sisters on the basic tenets of St. Thomas' philosophical and theological thought. Familiarity with St. Thomas' doctrine is one of the essential components of the Congregation's formation program, which was designed by Father Wladyslaw Kornilowicz and Foundress Mother Elizabeth Czacka and is described in the Constitutions of the Congregation.

In view of the nature of the proposal and my close ties and long-standing friendship with the Laskian community, I gladly accepted the invitation. Using the material accumulated in the first phase, I set about preparing the lecture series, which began in the spring of 1977. I completed the series just before Christmas of that year. It was a challenging task, given the extremely diverse audience that attended the sessions. Among the sisters who came to hear me were women with backgrounds in serious studies and with years of experience in teaching, pastoral work, and other areas; there were also young candidates and novices, as well as domestic sisters engaged entirely in practical occupations and having nothing in common with systematic philosophical or humanistic thought. A group of lay people also participated in the sessions. I presented each lecture at two sites, speaking first to an audience in Laski and then repeating the lecture for a group gathered at a convent on Piwna Street in Warsaw.

The difficulties arising from the great diversity in the audience's philosophical and theological preparation were overcome in basically two ways. First of all, I strove in my lectures to explain as fully and intelligibly as possible any difficult concepts and any views that seemed remote from everyday thinking. Next, the lectures were supplemented with meetings in which the material covered in my presentations was reviewed. These meetings were conducted on a regular basis at the Piwna Street convent by Sister Joanna Lossow, who has a master's in philosophy and a licentiate in theology, and at Laski by Sister Maria Janina Borkowska, an agricultural engineer, who also has a master's in philosophy. These sisters contributed greatly to the whole endeavor, since at those meetings participants could ask questions for which there was no time at the lectures —and clear up whatever difficulties they might be having.

The third stage consisted in the task of drafting the text of the lectures into book form. I was aided in this work by Sister Ruth Wosiek, who is a specialist in Polish studies and has a master's in theology, and by Thadeus Urbaniak, who has a master's in philosophy. I am very grateful to them for their help. Yet, despite this valuable and necessary assistance, the text was still not ready for publication, since it was based on the spoken word transcribed from tapes. I, therefore, decided to revise the whole text, but in such a way that the arrangement and content of the chapters in the book would closely correspond to the topics and inner structure of the lectures.

The views of St. Thomas are necessarily presented here in a succinct fashion, although I was careful to emphasize the most important and central points of his doctrine. It would have been impossible to treat all aspects of his doctrine with the same degree of completeness, and so I had to be selective in my choice of topics. I deal here in greater depth and detail with the philosophy of being, giving particular attention to the theological issues related to it, and also with the philosophical conception of the human being. On the other hand, I do not attempt in this book to go deeply into ethical questions (especially particular ethical issues), since that would require a separate extensive work. After all, St. Thomas devoted the largest part of the *Summa Theologiae* to particular ethical issues, the part called "The Second Part of the Second Part" (*Secunda Secundae*).

Every authentic philosophical view—and especially every great philosophical view—is always simultaneously transtemporal and historical. It is beyond time and space in the realm of its most profound and metaphysical concepts; it is also fully historical as a view that has arisen in a particular *hic et nunc* (which appears in all applications of metaphysics to various fields of study) and is received and reinterpreted in another *hic et nunc*. This book, too, presents the results of a new interpretation—made in new, 20th-century conditions—of the philosophical and theological reflections of a great 13th-century thinker and scholar. The reader shall be the judge of the degree to which the fruits of St. Thomas' reflections presented here are of lasting value, and also of the extent to which they are relevant for the present age.

For many years and from many quarters I have received requests for a concise and accessible presentation of an overview of the philosophy of Thomas Aquinas. I will be happy if this volume responds to that need. The need itself is an expression on the part of many sectors of a growing interest in classical philosophy and in the philosophical and theological thought of the great medieval period. We recognize today that over the centuries Thomism, which sought to be a doctrinal school faithful to St. Thomas' thought, in reality often betrayed that thought in many fundamental points. This gave rise to false interpretations of St. Thomas' philosophy that seriously distorted his thought. I hope this book, which aims at presenting St. Thomas' own views purged of all the accretions of the various kinds of "Thomism," will contribute to a better and more unbiased knowledge and understanding of those views. This is a necessary condition if their lasting and timely value is to shine forth.

Upon the publication of this book, I wish to thank all who have contributed—often at the cost of a great deal of effort and labor—to its appearance. I extend my sincere gratitude to the Franciscan Sisters, Servants of the Cross, whom I mentioned earlier by name, to Thadeus Urbaniak, and to my publisher ZNAK, not only for the part they played in the preparation of this book, but also for the climate of enormous goodwill that accompanied its emergence. My grateful thoughts also go out to two places with which this work is closely connected, the retreat house in Laski near Warsaw and the guest house of the Capuchin Friars in Tenczyn near Myslenice, where I found complete understanding, making it possible for me to do the final editing of the text in peace and quiet.

STEFAN SWIEZAWSKI

Warsaw—Tenczyn
September 1982

1

Why Philosophy?

Why should we concern ourselves with philosophy? Why St. Thomas? What we are really asking is this: Why, when life in the Congregation is already so hectic and filled with toil and trouble, should we encumber it still more with the kind of effort these lectures entail? And yet something very important is at stake here, something intimately connected with the spirituality of Laski. After all, doctrine—and doctrine understood contemplatively, not as a set of formulas but in terms of its very essence—is one of the three distinguishing marks of Laskian spirituality, both for the Congregation and for the local community. Franciscan love, the Benedictine liturgy, and doctrine—the thought of St. Thomas—these three things should converge in the works of Laski. That is what I always heard from the lips of Father Kornilowicz.

We find ourselves today in a rather difficult situation. In the present age to speak of this type of philosophy and to immerse ourselves in the thought of St. Thomas is certainly an activity that goes against the current, for the current surrounding us today is an anti-philosophical and largely anti-Thomistic current. But activity against the current—which could be called "trout-like" (since trout swim against the current)—is important, because through it we set ourselves in opposition to the diabolic mill that merely multiplies different functions and activities and leaves no room for reflection, quiet contemplation, and a deep look at reality. To draw near to the thought of St. Thomas is also in a sense to confront the prevailing tendencies in philosophy today, for in contemporary philosophical currents it is extremely difficult to discover what we have in mind when we speak of the need for philosophy in the Congregation and in Laski. First, then, I would like to explain what I think philosophy ought to be and why I believe your Congregation must concern itself with philosophy. Indeed, it may seem strange that the Franciscan Sisters, Servants of the Cross, are supposed to concern themselves with philosophical issues.

Let us first reflect upon the origin, or etymology, of the word "philosophy" itself. This is a Greek term, made up of two Greek words:

phileo, which means "I am a friend of," "I love," and *sophia*, which means "wisdom." We thus at once strike upon the heart of the matter: philosophy is simply—and ought to be simply—the development of a friendship with wisdom. This is very difficult to do and requires lifelong practice and effort. The value of wisdom, which, as we shall see, extends to every sphere, both natural and supernatural, and finds its fulfillment in the supernatural sphere, is so great that the author of the Book of Wisdom did not hesitate to pen these words about it:

> And so I prayed, and understanding was given me.
> I entreated, and the spirit of Wisdom came to me.
> I esteemed her more than scepters and thrones,
> and I held riches as nothing compared with her.
> I saw no priceless jewel as her peer,
> for next to her all gold is a pinch of sand
> and beside her silver seems like mud.
> I loved her more than health and beauty,
> and having her was for me greater than having light,
> since her radiance shines forth unceasingly.
> All good things came to me along with her,
> and I took riches without number from her hands.
> I delighted in all things, for Wisdom governed them all,
> but I did not know she was their mother.
> What I learned with a pure heart,
> I pass on without reserve;
> I will not hide her riches,
> for she is an inexhaustible treasure to us all.
> Those who have her win God's friendship,
> commended to God by the gifts of her teaching.
> May God grant me to speak as I should
> and think worthily of God's gifts to us,
> since God is the guide of Wisdom
> and God directs the wise.
> We are in God's hand, we ourselves and our words,
> together with all our understanding and technical skill.
> God gave me true knowledge of what things are,
> that I might know the structure of the world
> and the power of the elements,

the beginning and end of times, as well as their middle,
the alternation of the solstices and the changing of the seasons,
the course of the year and the positions of the stars,
the natures of animals and the instincts of wild beasts,
the powers of spirits and purposes of humans,
the varieties of plants and the virtues of roots:
All that is hidden, all that is manifest, I have come to know,
for I was taught by Wisdom, who made all things.
                                        (Wisdom 7:7–21)

This celebrated text has a complement in another text of the Old Testament in the Book of Job:

But where is wisdom to be found?
Where is the place of understanding?
The path to it is unknown to mortals;
it cannot be found in the land of the living.
"It is not in me," says the Abyss.
"Nor with me," says the Sea.
It cannot be bought with gold,
nor can its worth be weighed in silver.
It cannot be purchased with the gold of Ophir
or with precious onyx or sapphire.
Neither gold nor glass can match its worth,
nor can works of solid gold.
Coral and crystal are not even worthy of mention;
wisdom is more precious than pearls.
Topaz from Cush cannot compare with it,
and even the purest gold is no match for it.
But where does wisdom come from?
Where is understanding to be found?
It lies beyond the view of every living thing,
hidden from the birds of the air.
Perdition and Death say,
"We have heard of its renown."
God alone knows the path to wisdom
and where it is to be found.
For God sees to the ends of the earth,

and observes all that lies under the heavens.
When God set the weight of the wind
and gave the waters their measure,
when God made the law for the rain
and the path of the lightening,
God then saw wisdom and assessed it,
considered it and fathomed it.
And God said to humanity,
"The fear of the Lord is wisdom,
and the avoidance of evil is understanding."
(Job 28:12–28)

These texts are a classic avowal of the grandeur and greatness of wisdom, a wisdom that is twofold: natural and supernatural. We should pray for wisdom, for through wisdom we find truth, and truth is a value just as important as love. Truth is not a lower value than love: they are interchangeable values. Moreover, wisdom is and ought to be attainable by all. To be wise one need not necessarily be well educated. Occasionally, learning even stands in the way of wisdom. Indeed, wisdom sometimes implants itself far better in a simple soul, because a certain simplicity of spirit is a condition of wisdom. And so at times wisdom takes root in a simple, uncomplicated, not overly complex person rather than in one who is learned and filled with constraints and complexities.

Another important point is that without wisdom there is no holiness. Wisdom is a necessary condition of holiness—so says St. Thomas. That means it is a matter of grave consequence. All of us should grow in wisdom and pray fervently for this gift. Wisdom is, after all, one of the most important gifts of the Holy Spirit. While awaiting the gift of wisdom, we should do all we can, with all our natural powers and resources, to acquire the natural wisdom that prepares the ground for receiving the supernatural gift. And if we are all meant to partake of wisdom, then we should all concern ourselves with philosophy, since philosophy is friendship with wisdom. Just as St. Thomas said that wisdom is a necessary condition of holiness, someone in the 15th century (Pico della Mirandola) observed in a similar vein that anyone who does not engage in philosophy is not even a human being. Philosophy is a necessary condition of humanness; in order to be a human being, in order to develop our humanity, we must be friends of wisdom.

Yet, it does not seem realistic to expect everyone to engage in the study of something as difficult as philosophy.

To put the matter in this way, however, shows that we have a faulty notion of philosophy. We must draw a fundamental distinction between scientific and prescientific philosophy. Scientific philosophy, philosophy understood as a science, has, like every other science, its own terminology —a technical, formidable language all its own. It also has its own extensive and complicated history, a very broad history, embracing several thousands of years and all the races of the earth. European philosophy is only a small segment of the scientific philosophy produced by humankind.

On the one hand, then, there is scientific philosophy, which is in some respects extremely difficult. In addition to such scientific philosophy, however, which is a scientific system, a set of the tenets, arguments, and inquiries, along with certain great historical controversies that shed light on how such philosophy developed and matured over the centuries, there is another kind of philosophy, prescientific philosophy, which is not organized into a system, a set of tenets, etc. It is this latter, prescientific philosophy that should be engaged in by all. In this sense, Pico della Mirandola was right when he said that anyone devoid of philosophy is not a human being.

Prescientific philosophy is similar to what we call ordinary wisdom. It means knowing how to reflect, how to question, how to take a quiet, deep look at one thing or another. All of us to some degree engage in such prescientific philosophy. We begin to philosophize when we are seized by the wonder of a thing, and this wonder often leads to fascination. When Father Thadeus in Laski gazes at a plant, a flower, or a bird, he is philosophizing, because he is entranced by the creature's appearance, its habits, its delicate structure. This is not a purely aesthetic perusal, not simply a fascination with the beautiful world—but something more. And that is why Plato, one of the world's greatest philosophers, said that philosophy begins in wonder. Wonder is the source of philosophizing, and the simplest things can awaken this wonder in us.

Such wonder is most frequently found in little children. Jesus said in the Gospel: *unless you become like children* (Matt. 18:3). One could say that *unless you become like children*—you will not be able to philosophize. Not only *will you not enter the reign of heaven*, but you will not be able to philosophize, because the most truly profound and genuine wonder appears in a child at the philosophical age, which comes before the rational age when the child already begins to reason. The age of four, five, six—that is the time when children ask the most perplexing questions, which we often do not answer because we do not want to plunge into the depths of reality with the child. Yet, we ought to swim out into those depths and allow the child fully to develop.

Our whole culture—a culture abloom in technology and comfort—is the result of an education based not on the philosophical age, which is the beginning of wisdom, but rather on the subsequent rational age, when the child has already begun to reason, and reasoning is not the same as philosophical reflection. It is in those first questions, which are an expression of fascination and wonder over little things, things we tend to overlook, that the philosophical attitude takes its point of departure. It makes no difference whether we wonder at the whole of reality, the whole world, or at some living organism, or at some tiny internal structure, or at some aspect of life. Every fragment of our surrounding reality is by nature capable of evoking fascination and wonder in us.

Years ago I wrote an article about philosophy and its various forms and functions, and in it I said that *the task of philosophy is not to improve life, and yet it is an irrefutable fact that philosophy is one of the factors that most effectively contributes to this improvement.*[1] Philosophy is not simply a rule of life; it is not replete with directives telling us how to behave. And yet, if properly pursued, philosophy elevates and deepens both our intellectual culture and our practical culture, both our way of thinking and our way of acting.

Philosophy was once given a rather peculiar name. In the Platonic school, philosophy was called a *meditatio mortis*, a reflection on death. This does not refer to some gloomy preoccupation with the fact that everything must end, that nothing endures, that the end is near, and so on. That is not what is at issue here, but rather something altogether different, namely, that philosophy, when properly pursued, is a school that teaches us that only mortification brings forth life, that there is no life without mortification, without the dying away of certain elements so that others might grow. And this is something that has tremendous importance for the whole of life and for the whole of asceticism in the best sense of the term. This is the school that allows us to choose and trains us in properly apprehending a scale of values, a school that constantly promotes the improvement of life.

This *meditatio mortis*, or reflection on death, is based on the fact that we must constantly—from the beginning of our conscious existence to its final moment—make choices, choices that are reflective, thoughtful choices, because they always involve choosing between a greater good and a lesser good, and the lesser good must die away for the greater one to grow. That is what it means to meditate on death in a manner that fosters and deepens life. By cultivating in ourselves the ability to wonder and the capacity to assess values properly, we nurture wisdom from the natural side, through our own effort. Wisdom in its highest form is, as I said, a gift "from above," but philosophy in the most proper sense of the term is the nurturing of wisdom, the pursuit of wisdom, "from below." We are all called to prescientific philosophy, which is, in a sense, necessarily theological, open to the question of the Absolute, the question of the unconditional and highest value, the question of ultimate things—open to God.

As we take our first steps in philosophy, in wisdom, we learn to contemplate. Philosophy is simply the school of natural contemplation. We are accustomed to speaking of contemplation only in the sense of the prayerful contemplation that leads us toward mystical experience—in other words, only in the sense of supernatural contemplation. There is however, also a natural contemplation, which essentially is not yet prayer but a preparation for the prayerful "gaze." It is a contemplation that I would call introductory and incomplete, a preparatory contemplation, one that is necessary to make it possible for the other to be able to develop fully within us.

If our contemporary culture makes it so difficult for us to hear the voice of the Gospel, that is because we lack the ears to hear and the eyes to see. We do not have the complete preparation that education in the family and school should provide from the very start. For centuries now we have ceased being developed in the spirit of the primacy of wisdom and have been being formed only in the spirit of the primacy of technology, the primacy of usefulness, convenience, comfort. Our European culture has lost so very much in comparison with, for example, certain Eastern or African cultures. The development of the particular sciences, technology, and comforts has been bought at an incredibly great price—the loss of the values of wisdom and contemplation.

The vocation of every Christian, including those engaged in temporal affairs, is to cultivate the contemplative life and to cultivate it, as René Voillaume says, *au coeur des masses*[2] (*in the heart of the crowd*), in the very tumult of life, in the center of everything going on around us, in the bustle of our commitments and concerns. And for this very reason philosophy as the school of contemplation and wisdom is essential for everyone. It is what I would call the true school of life.

If, however, we look for such philosophy among contemporary philosophical currents, our search will be in vain. The development of Western culture has led systematic, scientific philosophical thought to go in a direction other than wisdom—and it will take an enormous effort to reverse this course. We shall repeatedly have to go way back in time, not just tens but even hundreds of years, to find in our intellectual heritage the kinds of values that can serve as guides for us in the present age. Where shall we find such a school of philosophy, such a teacher? Moreover, we want the wisdom that we learn and acquire to be a universal wisdom, one suitable for all times and all cultures. The problem of this selection and this quest is a very difficult one indeed.

The Second Vatican Council is commonly viewed as a pastoral council, one that seemingly forgot all about philosophy. So it is said, but this is a misguided interpretation of the Council's works and achievements. Vatican II, in its Pastoral Constitution *The Church in the Modern World*, expresses these very important words concerning the need (I shall quote the Latin text) *servandi apud homines facultates contemplationis ac admirationis, quae ad sapientiam adducunt*—the need to reconcile contemporary culture *with the preservation in human beings of the capacity for contemplation and wonder, which lead to wisdom* (*Gaudium et Spes* 56). Although the conciliar text does not designate it as such, these words contain the agenda of philosophy. If we fail to awaken in future generations the ability to contemplate and wonder, we shall be swallowed up by those cultures that still manage to attend to these values and to develop them creatively.

This, then, is why philosophy is needed, why we all need it, and why it is especially needed in Laski. This is also why, in our pursuit of philosophy, we choose St. Thomas as our guide.

2

Why St. Thomas?

St. Thomas lived in the 13th century. For our present purposes, a few words about his life will suffice. Several years ago, in 1974, we celebrated the 700th anniversary of his death. He was a Dominican, and in those days being a Franciscan or a Dominican was like being a "Christian hippie." The mendicant orders were not in step with the respectable and long-established congregations of the day. Thomas was a great saint and a superb teacher; he was extremely well-disciplined inwardly, and he wrote so clearly that, if you know Latin, it is much easier to read his own works than to read any of his commentators. He was a great theologian and one of the greatest philosophers.

When, however, we turn to his thought today and attempt to base our intellectual formation on it, we hear voices of protest from many sides, and even from within ourselves. How could someone who pursued scientific philosophy and theology in a time so remote from our own, someone affected by so many conditions radically different from those in which we live, have anything of concrete value and significance to say to us today? This is the sort of question one frequently hears. Is it possible, though, to speak of "the end of Thomistic Catholicism," the end of Catholicism based on St. Thomas' thought and expounded upon by his commentators? Is this in fact the case? What has ended? What survives and should survive? Those who regard St. Thomas with a certain resistance and aversion generally do not take into account all that has occurred in the area of Thomistic studies over the past thirty years or so. They tend to rely mainly on research and findings from the years prior to 1939.

What kinds of objections are most frequently raised?

One commonly asked question is, How can philosophical thought from the 13th century have anything of genuine value to offer us in the late 20th century? Is such a thing even possible?

If philosophy—and I am speaking now of scientific philosophy—developed in the same way the other sciences do (e.g., the natural sciences), then St. Thomas' philosophy would certainly have to be discarded, just as, for example, different types of physics that have appeared since medieval times down to the present have had to be discarded. First came the collapse of Aristotelian physics, which was a certain hypothesis—and a rather interesting one—explaining physical reality. It collapsed in the face of experimental research and was replaced by other views, which crystallized into mechanistic physics. For a long time it seemed as though mechanistic physics was the absolute and final view, but then around the turn of the 20th century its shortcomings also came to light. The need for the creation of a new theory became apparent, because experimental research had developed and precision in measurement had improved to such a degree that the old interpretation became inadequate. And so quantum physics and the theory of relativity took their turn in replacing the old views. Such, then, were the hypotheses and theories that arose one after another, only to be supplanted after a time by new ones. New observations, new measurements, and new and improved experiments are continually being made, and so there will always be a need for new theories to explain them.

If St. Thomas' philosophy—as is often falsely maintained—were dependent upon the theories of nature prevalent in his day, then it would have to be rejected along with those obsolete theories. If, for example, it turned out that St. Thomas' philosophy were so closely connected with Aristotelian physics that, with the collapse of that physics, it would no longer have any justification, then we would certainly have to regard it as outdated. We know today that this is indeed the case with respect to certain parts of St. Thomas' thought, particularly his philosophy of nature. In this area, St. Thomas relied on the physics of his day. For us, therefore, his philosophizing on this topic is misguided and naive, simply because it is connected to a theory of physics that today is obsolete. There are, then, certain areas, certain parts, of St. Thomas' thought that we may regard as essentially irrelevant for our time.

The works he wrote on philosophical anthropology that have to do with physiology have also lost their relevance, since the investigation of the natural phenomena with which they deal has progressed to such a degree that today those phenomena look entirely different from the way they looked seven centuries ago, or even a hundred years ago. And so the parts of St. Thomas' thought that are in some way strictly dependent upon matters of this sort are also obsolete. Similarly, certain sociological concepts in St. Thomas' social ethics, to the extent that they are linked to a discussion of a feudal system that has long since ceased to exist, can have no contemporary application.

But—and this is a very important *but*—I have been speaking here of applications or adaptations of philosophical thought, and not of its very essence. Philosophical thought itself, the pure contemplation of reality, is not affected by temporal change. With regard to reality, by virtue of the wonder and fascination mentioned earlier, we philosophize today in the same way people did in ancient or medieval times.

It is very important to realize that the development of philosophical thought does not resemble the development of the particular sciences, such as the natural sciences mentioned above, but is much more like the development of the arts. For example, classical achievements in the architectural arts do not grow old. The value of Egyptian or Greek architecture is absolutely inviolable, even though it developed many hundreds or even thousands of years ago. Art, when it attains a certain purity and perfection, such that it takes on the attributes of the classical achievements, transcends time and becomes eternally young. The beauty of a Doric column will always be beautiful; it is something that absolutely cannot grow old. The more a thing embodies those great classical values, the more it is eternally young. Just as the philosophical life resembles the life of genuine art, it also resembles the inner life. It would be absurd to suggest that the achievements of the inner life of St. Paul the Apostle, or St. Francis of Assisi, or St. Catherine of Siena, or St. Theresa of Avila are out of date. The essence of their achievements, of their mystical experiences, is absolutely transtemporal.

In all great philosophical thought, therefore, there are certain parts that, like the philosophy of nature, philosophical anthropology, or social philosophy, are dependent on spatiotemporal conditions. At the same time, however, in all authentic philosophy, in the legacy of every great philosopher, there is also a group of the kinds of ideas, the kinds of thoughts, the kinds of views that transcend time. Whatever remains eternally young also remains eternally relevant. This timeless core should be extracted from each philosophical view and should be revived and introduced into our present philosophical considerations. That is why St. Thomas—and this is the first fruit of these reflections—can be a guide for us, as can Plato, Aristotle, Buddha, and every other great thinker. Just as the music of Bach or the works of any great classical musician never grow old, neither do the authentic achievements of philosophical thought.

Let us now examine some of the particular charges made against Thomism and first try to understand certain difficulties people today have with St. Thomas' thought. It is said that Thomism is anti-ecumenical, that neither the East nor the West accepts it, that the Orthodox and Protestant churches have no liking for St. Thomas. But the question immediately arises whether this aversion is directed at St. Thomas or at Thomism. The answer is simple: at Thomism. Unfortunately, Thomism, the philosophy that developed under the banner of St. Thomas over the years, was in many cases very unfaithful to the most essential philosophical thoughts and intuitions of St. Thomas himself. In a similar way, what passed for an expression of the most perfect Christian culture was often contrary to authentic Christianity. I am, of course, referring here to the crusades, the crusaders, the conquest of new continents in the name of Jesus Christ, the proclamation that a Christian system was being established, and then the practice in it of torture and the like. We know only too well how often such things happen in the world.

Toward the end of the Middle Ages, Christendom, which was a kind of United Nations of its day, adopted Thomism as an ideology. This was detrimental both to St. Thomas and to Thomism. Thomism ceased being a search for and a contemplation of truth and became merely a set of directives, ostensibly intended to safeguard the possession of truth. I could understand those at the Vatican Council who were unsympathetic to Thomism, but I realized that they did not know how to differentiate between Thomism and St. Thomas, and they vented their antipathy toward this distorted Thomism on St. Thomas himself.

At an international conference held at the University of Louvain in 1974, I presented a paper entitled "On the Distortions of St. Thomas' Thought in the Thomistic Tradition."[3] After my presentation, a Jesuit who had been living in India for many years came up to me and said that to approach the original sources, to approach St. Thomas, in this way and to present his pure and unadulterated thought was the best way to build a bridge between the philosophy and theology of the West and the Far East. If the representatives of the Protestant world, at a time when it was difficult to be loyal to the church because there was so much in it that was evil —if they had known and understood St. Thomas well—things would certainly have turned out differently. Unfortunately, the encounter between Luther and Cajetan was tragic. Although Cajetan was one of the greatest commentators on St. Thomas, studies today reveal that he deviated in many points from the unadulterated thought of St. Thomas.

We also come across the charge that Thomism is an anachronism. Even when cleansed of all its 13th-century encrustations, it is still not in line with contemporary philosophy. It certainly does not conform to that "line." Thomism is "trout-like," as I said before. It can be described as "going against the current" in the sense that it is fundamentally opposed to the subjectivism, the concentration on the self, that, unfortunately, characterizes all modern European philosophical thought. Contemporary philosophy, instead of being a reflection on reality as a whole, wherein we ourselves are also situated, is becoming—as David Hume called it—*an inquiry concerning human understanding*, a reflection on the world of our products; it is becoming a philosophy of culture, a philosophy of what we create, and not a philosophy of reality itself. One could say that the predominant feature of contemporary philosophical thought is that it is incapable of going beyond the sphere of the enchanted circle of the subject, of subjectivity, of the self. St. Thomas' mode of thought is the most radical medicine for this subjectivistic, egocentric mode of thought.

In this connection, it would be worth reading even a single chapter of the interesting memoirs of Father Rzewuski, a Dominican priest.[4] Rzewuski, who was once a very popular and successful artist and the epitome of a "man of the world," suddenly became a Dominican, went through the rigorous school of the Dominican novitiate, and later described his spiritual conversion. He had been raised in the spirit of the philosophy of Kant, one of the greatest philosophers, who took as the chief principle of his philosophy the notion that when we know, we do not know reality, but only impose our own subjective categories on the surrounding world. This is the very quintessence of subjectivism. Father Rzewuski writes of how extremely difficult it was for him to change and accept the school of St. Thomas, because he had to make a complete reversal and go from subjectivism to objectivism, to objective thinking; he had to attend to what was beyond the self. This return to objective reality seems to me to be just what we need to cure what ails us today. Though the journey is extremely arduous and difficult, it is also the best school of the inner life. From this point of view, all subjectivisms are a serious evil; the more we forget ourselves, the closer we are to God.

A final charge leveled against a Thomistic formation is that this kind of objective thought isolates us from real life. People brought up on St. Thomas are said to be insensitive to the poor of this world, incapable of concerning themselves with anything oppressive, anything disturbing, in the world around us. Supposedly, those who are schooled in the realm of objective thought cease to understand the tragedies and vicissitudes of human life and shut themselves up in their own "ivory towers." They contemplate, they reflect, they wonder, but they steer clear of the spiritually and materially destitute masses.

Philosophy may indeed have such a formative effect on a person if it is not directed toward real existence—I will say more about this later. Here let it suffice to say that there are philosophies that focus only on the question, What is this? What kind of thing is this?—and do not concern themselves with the fact that something is, that something exists. Philosophies that abstract from existence abstract from reality itself, and these are the ones that can lock us up in an ivory tower. But such philosophizing is certainly not the philosophizing of St. Thomas.

In any case, the people themselves who were formed in the objective philosophy, theology, and mysticism of St. Thomas are the best response to the charge of isolationism. Wladyslaw Kornilowicz, Jacques Maritain, Charles Journet, and René Voillaume were all people formed in this way. Would it not be a terrible injustice to say of them that they were insensitive to the poor of the world? The very fact that Father Kornilowicz chose to work in Laski and not somewhere else is a sufficient response to the charge in his case. At the same time, philosophy is not meant to concern itself directly with matters that make up the tumult of human adversity, but is meant to form us in such a way that we will be sensitive to the whole of reality. The accusation of insensitivity to the poor of the world applies to a very profound distortion of Thomism, and not to the full and authentic thought of Thomas himself.

Above all, his thought is fundamentally theocentric: it directs everything toward God and places God at the center of all concerns. Father Alexander Fedorowicz wrote beautifully about this issue in an article in *Tygodnik Powszechny* commemorating Cardinal Journet.[5] What he basically said was this: I am not concerned here with who is right about Thomism or St. Thomas, but I do know one thing, that the people with whom I am acquainted who were educated in this way were people like Cardinal Journet and others like him, and—he concluded—it is clear that this formation is what gave them the kind of attitude they had toward life.

And so we can today take St. Thomas as our teacher and guide in philosophical formation. But he does not provide us with, nor do we expect him to be able to provide us with, a ready-made formula for how we should live and act—that is not the point. He will teach us philosophical contemplation, and this will have a formative influence in shaping our whole culture. I believe that such a formation would finally give us what we so badly need: those eyes to see and ears to hear. It would be a step toward making our culture—which would then be no longer individualistic but social—more a culture of wisdom than merely a culture of science and particular knowledge.

Relevant in this regard is a letter from Paul Claudel, one of the greatest poets of our times, to Father Ernest Friche in 1928.[6] Claudel was then the French ambassador to the United States, and he wrote that people were asking him whether he was a Thomist, whether he was a follower of St. Thomas. This was his response: *Following my conversion, my first confessor was constantly encouraging me to study St. Thomas. Above all, he advised me not to read any commentaries, any introductions, but to attack the works of St. Thomas directly. I could not have received better advice... The commentaries probably would have caused me to detest St. Thomas. Instead of commentaries, I set about reading his works in 1895, after my departure for China. I felt as if I were exploring a new land, getting acquainted with some virgin territory, a completely unfamiliar country. I learned the Scholastic language just as one learns English—in the course of using it—and, after a hundred pages or so, I could easily follow this wonderfully clear thought. In this way, I read through both Summas, finishing my reading before returning to France in 1899. It was an extremely refreshing and exceptional exercise for my mind.* He then wrote of how much this contributed to his own creativity, and said: *You are, therefore, completely correct in calling me a Thomistic poet, because the Thomistic principles have been fused, so to speak, into every movement of my artistic life.*

3

St. Thomas' Productivity

Now that we have raised two preliminary questions fundamental for our discussion—Why philosophy? and Why St. Thomas?—and attempted to respond to them, I shall give a brief description of St. Thomas' productivity, so that we can then take up a very important issue, namely, the relation of natural knowledge to supernatural knowledge.

First we must enter the terrain of the history of philosophy. Readers with no background in philosophy and its history should familiarize themselves at least in a cursory way with the first volume of *The History of Philosophy* by Wladyslaw Tatarkiewicz, or some similar text. It would be good to do a little reading in this area in order to become familiar with certain concepts that will keep coming up in the course of our reflections.

When we speak of philosophy and its history, we should have in mind the whole of humankind—not just that small segment of it that was brought up on Greco-Latin culture. Great philosophy was produced by the Far East, by India, and also by China. These cultures are much older than our own. Although we are their "younger siblings," we ourselves were brought up on a philosophy that came from the basin of the Mediterranean Sea, and this is the philosophy that interests us most, especially that which arose from the roots of Greek philosophy and found its way into our own time.

Every complete philosophy is basically religious. The first great Greek thinkers were not materialists in the strict sense of the word. While it is true that they did not know how to arrive at a clear conception of spirit and God, yet they sought God in all their philosophy. There were basically two issues that fascinated the Greek philosophers. One was the desire to explain the tension between constancy and change. Change, motion, is one of the phenomena that we humans find most intriguing. Already as children we are most interested in what moves, in the fact that changes are taking place. In philosophizing we arrive at questions concerning the causes of change. This inquiry into the causes of change ultimately leads to the question of God, to one unchanging principle. The Greek philosophers wondered about what is permanent in the surrounding world and what passes away. The arrangements of certain elements pass away, they said, but the elements themselves endure. According to Plato, for example, the world we perceive with our senses is transient, and what he called Ideas are permanent; Ideas are the unchanging archetypes of all transitory things. We will return again to these questions to see how they were dealt with by Aristotle, a student of Plato. Thus, the first of the two great problems that interested the Greek philosophers was an explanation of the phenomenon of motion or change, the fact that everything changes, everything is in constant flux. In the face of such universal change and passing away, is there anything immutable and enduring?

The second problem is connected with human beings, with the human condition, with suffering. It can be summed up in the question, What is true happiness? The question of happiness is intimately connected with the problem of suffering. What must we do to abolish, master, or overcome suffering? Happiness was the other topic introduced by Greek philosophy. These two themes—motion (or change) and happiness (and suffering)— caused Greek thought to oscillate between a philosophy directed toward the world and a philosophy concerned primarily with human beings. These two great questions formed the axis upon which virtually all ancient philosophy revolved.

On the topic of human happiness, each of the ancient philosophical schools proposed its own "program of life." Some said, in a way reminiscent of the Hindu sages, that we will be happy only when we have ourselves under perfect control. This is what the Stoics taught. For them the ideal was to be insensitive to everything; to be wise and happy, we must be indifferent to everything that happens around us. Others believed that happiness consists in knowing how to take advantage of every moment, though not in the sense of indulgence in crude sensory pleasures, but in the sense of the art of experiencing every delight that comes our way. The Epicureans held this view. Still others said: avoid getting involved in any political, philosophical, or social concerns; if you want to be happy, merely observe life and do not get involved in it, because every involvement brings with it a thousand difficulties. This advice came from the Skeptics.

In the view of these ancient schools, philosophy appears as a program of life. Christianity was also called a philosophy by the first Christian writers of the 2nd century. For them Christianity was a philosophy in the sense that it was a school—a school of happiness and a school of life—

that offered the only real program for a true mastery of suffering and reconciliation with the fact of death. St. Justin, a 2nd-century martyr, who went through a number of philosophical schools of thought, tells of how he eventually met a learned hermit, a wise man, who taught him the philosophy of Christ, and of how the philosophy of Christ became for him the one philosophical school he could fully accept.

In the first centuries of Christianity, this Christian philosophy appears to have totally eclipsed all other philosophies. Testimony of the resurrection, victory over death, and a unique prescription for happiness paved the way to Christianity for one and all, the most learned as well as the most simple. At that time—this is a short digression, to which I shall later return—the hardest thing for philosophers to accept was the truth of the resurrection. They found it much easier to acknowledge the immortality of the human soul, the spiritual nature of the soul, than the resurrection, because in those days a Neoplatonic form of Plato's philosophy held sway, and in it the spiritual element reigned supreme. Consequently, the issue of the spiritual nature of the human being was not a problem. The body, on the other hand, was regarded as such a worthless aspect of the human being, as something so despicable, that Christianity, which proclaimed the great dignity of matter and of the body, the Incarnation and the Resurrection, was a scandal for the people of that time. The earliest apologists—Athenagoras, Justin, and others—encountered their greatest difficulties in proclaiming and defending the resurrection, the real resurrection, of both Christ and every human being. This is an example of the kinds of difficulties that confronted philosophical reflection at the boundary of faith and philosophy. As Christian thought developed, it would be in constant dialogue, in continual debate, with ancient pagan thought.

The great Greek and Latin doctors of the Church are, up to a certain point in history, called "Fathers," and they were indeed true Fathers of the Church. Their writings are called "patristic," from the Latin word *patres* (fathers). The Greek and Latin Fathers, the greatest of whom was St. Augustine, shaped the early foundations of Christian thought. There was no attempt in those days to distinguish philosophy from theology; the sole concern of Christian thinkers was to reflect upon the truths of the Gospel.

St. Augustine went through several non-Christian philosophical schools of thought. For a long time he was a skeptic, thinking that nothing could be known with certainty. Then for a number of years he was a follower of the Manichaean religion, a sect that believed in the existence of two first principles, two equally powerful elements—evil and good—in conflict with one another. The struggle of these two opposing elements was thought to determine the whole spiritual history of the world. Manichaeism, which was a dangerous distortion of Christianity, also failed to satisfy St. Augustine, and so he turned to Platonic thought. He was attracted by the primacy of the spiritual element that characterized Neoplatonism. Neoplatonism was a philosophical view that placed an excessive and radically conceived emphasis on the spiritual element in the human being and, in general, in reality as a whole. That is why Neoplatonism presented such an obstacle to an acceptance of the Resurrection and the Incarnation, the greatest realistic truths of the Christian faith.

Up until the time of St. Thomas all medieval thought was dominated by Neoplatonism, christianized in various ways. As a result, a radical spiritualism, a radical spirituality in Christian thought, together with a certain contempt for the bodily element, characterized the main currents of the philosophical and theological thought of the whole medieval period preceding St. Thomas. It would be a mistake to think that the predominant philosophy in that epoch was the thought of Aristotle, a student of Plato, since that situation arose only later, in St. Thomas' time.

It would be well to remember that in those days Latin Europe was, from a cultural point of view, about a hundred years behind the Arabian and Jewish worlds. The Arabs were then experiencing an enormous cultural expansion. This was a period in which the Arabian world was consolidating itself and developing, creating magnificent centers of thought and science. Baghdad in the East, Cordoba and Toledo in Spain, the North African territories—these were the regions in which the Arabian world was undergoing dynamic cultural development, both materially and, above all, spiritually. And so the crusaders during their expeditions did not encounter barbarians, but met with a world that was on a significantly higher cultural plane than their own; this should always be kept in mind. The Arabian culture fascinated the European Christian peoples. They realized that, although the Arabs were infidels, they were also the ones who had created such a marvelous, highly sophisticated culture.

Philosophy held a very lofty position in the Arabian world of that day. Theology and the distinctive mysticism of the Koran were at a high level. The particular sciences, too, especially the mathematical and natural sciences, were then being energetically developed in the Arabian world.

Mention should be made here of a place that stirs the heart of all who have an ecumenical soul—a beautiful city in Spain, the renowned Toledo. This is a city where something very rare in the history of humanity took place. There, over a significant part of the 12th century, a hundred years before St. Thomas' time, Christian, Moslem, and Jewish leaders worked together side by side in peace and harmony, though wars were raging all around. We have here a unique example of ecumenism in practice. The most magnificent works were produced there, translations from Arabic to Hebrew, from Hebrew to Latin. That was when the ideal of an educated person as one who knows three languages arose. Those three languages were conceived in a slightly different way from how they later came to be understood: not Greek, Hebrew, and Latin, but Arabic, Hebrew, and Latin. These three languages were, in fact, the key to the genuine knowledge of that era. Unfortunately, this creative cooperation did not last very long. As is always the case in human history, the sword, war, and barbarity destroyed that magnificent center, which to this day, however, is a model of how scientific and religious cooperation ought to look.

Something very remarkable also occurred, however, in the 13th century. Through the translations of the previous century, another great Greek philosopher, one rivaling Plato, found his way onto European soil— Aristotle, but an Aristotle that was not the authentic Greek Aristotle. It was an Arabian Aristotle, one annotated by the Arabs and handed down in their interpretation, which was not wholly in keeping with the original Aristotle and which, moreover, presented a great doctrinal danger to the Christian faith. Yet, this was the philosopher who most appealed to the minds of the time. It often happens in history that certain great figures suddenly become like the sun, fascinating everyone. This is just how Aristotle affected the people of the 13th century, especially the young.

Although Aristotle accepted the existence of God, his God was not a Providence, or, if a Providence, then not a Providence of the particular, but one who only watches over general things, genera and species, and not particular, concrete things. Aristotle, thus interpreted, also maintained that there was something divine in humans, but he did not accept the notion of individual immortality. He said that it is not the individual human soul that survives but only the spirit of humanity; humanity is immortal, not individual human beings.

Individual freedom and responsibility were also undermined in this interpretation of Aristotelianism; determinism and necessity reigned, including the notion that all events in the world were dependent upon the arrangements of the stars. The latter view had an important application in religion, one that took the form of a "horoscope of religions." The different religions were said to have arisen as a result of the appearance of certain arrangements of the stars. Christianity was also seen as one of the religions that, as theosophy would later say, come and go in the course of human history.

We can see, therefore, what great dangers to the Christian faith lurked in the "Arabian" Aristotelianism that had such a strong intellectual appeal. At the same time, scientific life was still at a primitive stage. Not only were philosophy and theology not differentiated from one another, but in St. Augustine the boundary between these sciences was purposely blurred. Neoplatonism, from which St. Augustine drew abundantly, in principle did not separate philosophy and theology. The particular sciences were also not set off from one another, and there was no awareness of the historical development of thought. Given such a state of affairs, it is not surprising that the church could become alarmed. After all, certain matters fundamental to the faith were at stake: Providence, individual immortality, moral responsibility, free will, and the uniqueness and divine nature of Christianity. These truths were challenged and questioned.

The church was also threatened by other serious dangers, such as the temporal power of the papacy and the materialistic attitudes of the clergy, along with their abject intellectual and moral condition. Pope Innocent III's dream about St. Francis was fully warranted. The pope saw in a dream that the structure of the church was deeply cracked from top to bottom, and that this Little Beggar would keep it from collapsing and fortify its bonds. No doubt St. Dominic also sensed and understood the same thing, perhaps even more profoundly from the intellectual side. The purity of the faith for St. Dominic and fidelity to the Gospel for St. Francis were what would decide the fate of the church. These principles found expression in the powerful movement of mendicant orders. St. Thomas was a part of the great evangelical renewal movement that appeared in the 13th century. The mendicant movement influenced the most important aspects surrounding the early stages and subsequent course of his life.

Thomas came from a great noble family that was related by marriage to the imperial family. The Counts of Aquino were powerful feudal lords in southern Italy. Thomas was born in 1224, and his parents, as often happened in those days, designated this very promising and gifted child for the priesthood, with the idea that he would someday, with their support, become the abbot of the most powerful abbey in that part of Italy, Monte Cassino. With this in mind, they sent him to the Benedictines at Monte Cassino as an oblate. Biographers say that the young Thomas would walk in the mountains there—and anyone who has been to Monte Cassino knows what magnificent distant views unfold from those hills—and constantly return to the question, What is God? This was the only problem that really interested Thomas. And precisely in this is the whole of his greatness revealed.

Thomas very soon came into conflict with his family. He had no intention of remaining with the Benedictines. He was drawn instead to what might be called the "hippies" of his day—the Dominicans and the Franciscans. Contrary to the aims and wishes of his family, he was attracted to a completely new congregation of friars called the Order of Preachers, who were a scandal to the hierarchical ecclesiastical institution of that time. An order whose livelihood depended on begging seemed an outrage. Thomas overcame many obstacles and entered the order of St. Dominic in Naples.

It is both significant and interesting that St. Thomas spent his youth and early years of study in Naples. Frederick II, a fierce enemy of the papacy, decided to organize a "second university"—the antithesis of the University of Paris, which was the first university, one subordinated to papal purposes—and to create in Naples a school in which Arabian science could develop without restraint. In this "pagan" university, which had excellent instructors, Thomas pursued his studies. This was all very providential because, as a result, he became acquainted with a "nonclerical" and to some extent anti-Christian concept of a university different from the papal concept. He also came to know the difficulties of those who studied there and who sought to attain genuine knowledge.

When Father Jacek Woroniecki spoke of St. Thomas, he would contrast him to Kant. Kant, that great philosopher who cast his shadow over virtually the whole of the 19th and 20th century, never stirred from the misty, gloomy city of Königsberg, and only with a precision to the very minute would he take a walk through its streets. Thomas, on the other hand, roamed about a great deal. Kant's critical philosophy and Thomas' realism are, according to Father Woroniecki, a reflection of these two so very different lifestyles. Thomas, on mule or on foot, as people traveled in those days, in his short, extremely industrious life, crossed the length and breadth of Europe several times over: Cologne, Paris, and Naples marked out the triangle of his numerous trips.

It is also significant that Thomas had an exceptional teacher, one of the greatest scholars of the era, Albert of Cologne, called "the Great," a German Dominican who introduced Thomas to the secrets of intellectual work. St. Thomas' whole intellectual life was a virtual battle. *Human life is a battle*; so, too, the intellectual life. Thomas fought on at least three fronts, and with each of his opponents he debated or battled in an ecumenical way, in the sense spoken of in the words of St. Paul: *I became all things to all people* (1 Cor. 9:22). St. Thomas' approach was always first to find some common ground, and only then to engage in debate.

His first opponent was pagan, heterodoxical Aristotelianism, the view that held the most fascination for the intellect and that was the most threatening in the sphere of faith for the Christianity of that era. His second opponent was a backward, closed-minded, intellectual conservatism, which refused to go beyond the context or boundaries imposed by christianized Neoplatonism. This was a war with radical spiritualism. In the former case, the conflict was with a particular kind of Aristotelian materialism; in the latter, the battle was waged with a Christianity that tended to be identified with spiritualism. Such a distortion is very dangerous: Christianity is neither a spiritualism nor a materialism. The third front was St. Thomas' war with the worldly clergy, who resisted the notion of mendicant monasticism. This was a very fundamental issue. The whole Council of Lyons in 1274, the year of St. Thomas' death, was a virtual battlefield; there were those at that Council who wanted to completely exterminate two great monastic families: the Dominicans and the Franciscans.

These, then, were the three fronts on which St. Thomas had continually to do battle. Near the end of his life he was asked by the pope and his monastic superiors to return to Naples, and so he went there again and founded the Studium Generale, a Dominican university that functioned alongside Frederick II's imperial university. He was already seriously ill as he made his way to Naples, and, in this state of grave illness, he was summoned personally by the pope to the Council, which was to take place in Lyons. While traveling to the Council in compliance with the papal order, he died on March 7, 1274, in a Cistercian abbey in Fossanuova near Terracino.

This is not the place to praise St. Thomas' sanctity, but I do wish to draw attention to two of his many qualities. First of all, he had tremendous purity of thought, which was combined with purity in the strict sense, purity of heart in general. Secondly, he had an extraordinary sense of discipline and obedience. They say that when he heard the bell announcing the end of the lecture hour, he would stop in the middle of a sentence. He was so disciplined that he possessed an absolute and immediate receptivity to whatever he thought was right and he would submit to it.

His productivity was simply astounding. Thomas lived not quite fifty years, he put up with travels and troubles—only in his later years did he get a secretary—and still he did a remarkable amount of writing. All of his works were connected with his teaching, as was then common for instructors. He was twice engaged as a lecturer at the greatest university of his day. It was extremely rare for any teacher to be invited to Paris a second time, and Thomas was twice at the University of Paris. He lectured on the *Sentences*, a commonly used handbook of theology that every lecturer in theology had to discuss. He also composed a multitude of biblical commentaries. Let us not forget that St. Thomas believed a theologian must be a scripture scholar. He also wrote a series of "questions" (longer tracts on particular subjects), shorter discourses, or *opuscula*, and a large number of commentaries on Aristotle, because he wanted to present what seemed to him to be the most accurate interpretation of Aristotle.

His chief works are two summas. "Summa" means a summarizing, a gathering into a whole. First came the *Summa Contra Gentiles*—against the infidels, against the pagans; in fact, that is not what it is about. It is a summa based mainly on rational argumentation, on philosophical reflections. The *Summa Theologiae*, on the other hand, is a real summa. It is an unfinished work consisting of three parts, the second part of which is divided into two more parts. Thus, there is the first part (*Prima*, I), the first part of the second part (*Prima Secundae*, I–II), the second part of the second part (*Secunda Secundae*, II–II), and the third part (*Tertia*, III). The third part was interrupted at Question 90 by St. Thomas' sickness and death and was later completed by his secretary Reginald.

Where in all of this is philosophy? Apart from his commentaries on Aristotle, St. Thomas actually wrote no philosophical works. He did, however, introduce philosophy into all of his works, and it could be said that in St. Thomas we find the first attempt to clearly define the difference between philosophy and theology, as well as the difference between faith and mysticism. Not long ago, in our own day, Jacques Maritain, in his book *Distinguish to Unite, or The Degrees of Knowledge*,[7] showed how many degrees of knowledge there are. We know that both philosophy and theology are in a certain sense "arbitrary": many philosophical views can be formulated and different theological views can also arise. Faith, on the other hand, is absolutely permanent and unchanging, as are the truths of faith. We also know that the mystical life, the inner experience of God, takes place in a completely different realm, a different order. The differentiation of these different orders is characteristic of St. Thomas' works and fruitful for the development of his scientific methodology and scholarly productivity.

4

Natural Knowledge and Supernatural Knowledge

It is often said that knowledge and faith, or reason and faith, are opposites. And yet faith gives knowledge—it is knowledge. Despite all its weakness and uncertainty, faith is still the source of the deepest knowledge. There are actually two types of knowledge, natural and supernatural. Philosophy and science are forms of natural knowledge. The knowledge that comes to us through faith, which is a gift, is supernatural knowledge.

This matter is often oversimplified by some, who say the Gospel alone suffices! Christ came and gave us the most important truths. Why, then, should we study anything else, why read anything else, except the Scriptures? Why should we question, why should we draw knowledge from other sources, when we have at our disposal a source of knowledge such as this? It is also sometimes said that philosophy and science only confuse the mind, cause difficulties, and create doubts, and so it would be much better to lock up all the dark recesses of reason, throw away the key, and just believe blindly and live a good life. An appeal is often made to the authority of St. Paul, who, after all, clearly warned: *Do not be deceived by philosophy* (see Col. 2:8). Not infrequently, there are those who are tempted to say: Enough with these philosophers! Who needs them?

In the history of Christian thought, this type of anti-philosophical attitude appeared on more than one occasion. Such a position is called "fideism" (from *fides*, meaning "faith"). According to fideism, faith should develop at the expense of reason; as faith increases, reason and its truths should recede increasingly into the background. An extreme formulation that could be regarded as capturing the essence of fideism is the saying attributed to Tertullian, a writer who lived at the turn of the 3rd century: *Credo quia absurdum*—I believe in something because it is absurd. This saying implies a basic conflict, an incompatibility, between what I blindly believe and what reason tells me. There were periods in the history of European thought when the fideistic spirit became so strong that even reading the Bible was deemed superfluous. There is no need to read at all, say the fideists; there is no need to study—all this is unnecessary. We should simply live a good life and do good deeds; everything else is just a waste of time and a distortion of the true Christian life.

The matter, however, is much more complicated than it may appear. First of all, not everyone is a Christian and not everyone is a believer. There are multitudes of people who believe in religions other than Christianity, and many people have no religious beliefs at all. We should also bear in mind that today we of the white race are, from the perspective of our religious convictions, far worse off than people of color. We are more paganized despite our Christianity. In fact, the predominant trait of the white race in our time is neo-paganism. Even believers today are experiencing difficulties. Consequently, the "ostrich policy" of sticking one's head in the sand and trying not to see the problems is surely far from good.

Similarly, those who attempt to develop faith in opposition to the intellect, to reason, are just as misguided as those who seek to express their concern for supernature, for the supernatural, through a disdain for nature. We must continually make choices that involve us in choosing a greater good over a lesser good, and yet we do not thereby disparage the lower good, but acknowledge its value. Likewise, if we view faith as superior to rational knowledge, this does not give us the right to disparage reason, to trample upon the natural intellectual sphere.

Philosophy, as the school of natural contemplation, is essential for the full development of human nature. A faith that takes root in an underdeveloped human nature will always be somewhat lopsided. It will develop, but in a way that is discordant and incomplete, not firmly fixed in the soil in which it should take root.

This brings us face to face with a fundamental question. I want to stress its importance because it is a really basic matter for human culture. The question is, Can we, without the help of revelation, without the help of the truths of faith, arrive at a knowledge of God and of things divine? To acknowledge God, do we need to accept revelation, or are we capable of arriving at this basic truth without revelation, independently of it? This was a problem that deeply concerned St. Thomas, since he was forever returning to the question, What is God?

This issue is of vital significance for our own culture. Are those most basic truths that are necessary for salvation accessible only through revelation, or are at least some of them attainable by reason? The same St.

Paul who was quite justified in saying *do not be deceived by philosophy* (since he was referring to both Neoplatonic hyper-spiritualism and materialistic tendencies) also clearly said in his Letter to the Romans that, by observing the natural world, it is possible to arrive at a knowledge of God (see Rom. 1:20).

St. Thomas in his "smaller summa," the *Summa Contra Gentiles*, says that in this work he is approaching questions *secundum quod ad cognitionem divinarum naturalis ratio per creaturas pervenire potest* (*Contra Gent*. IV, 1, 9): he is considering all questions from the point of view of whether *naturalis ratio*, natural reason, our natural power of cognition, unillumined by faith—*per creaturas*, through the observation of creatures, through the observation of the world, through contemplation (all of this is included in the phrase *per creaturas*)—can arrive *ad cognitionem divinarum*, at a knowledge of things divine. Is the human intellect limited to knowing only such precise realities as the world of mathematics or physics and such natural matters as the facts of experience, history, or nature—while revelation deals with all the rest? Is the intellect alone, the human being alone, capable of attaining at least in some respect and to some degree those ultimate things, that "all the rest"?

St. Thomas examines this question and responds in the following way: God has revealed those basic truths because it is difficult for us to arrive at them on our own; it is difficult for us to ascertain with complete certainty that God exists, that God is one, that God is a spirit, a person, and so on. These are extremely complex problems. We know how easy it is, if one already has some concept of the Absolute, for it to turn into something vague, polytheistic, impersonal, nonspiritual; how easy it is, for example, to go from the worship of God to the worship of the sun. We know—and history confirms this—how imperceptibly one can slide into a pantheistic concept of God and identify God with the world.

Now, among the truths of faith, among the truths necessary for salvation, says St. Thomas, speaking as a theologian, there are truths that we can arrive at with our own natural powers, but, he adds, it is good that they have also been revealed. St. Thomas refers to these truths by a Latin term difficult to render in another language: *revelabilia* (from *revelare*, meaning "to reveal"). They are truths that should be revealed but do not have to be revealed. In addition, says St. Thomas, among the truths of faith necessary for salvation there are other truths that cannot be arrived at without revelation, such as the Incarnation, the Trinity, and a number of others. These are called *revelata*, truths that must be revealed, for they cannot be attained in any other way. The distinction between *revelabilia* and *revelata* is very important.

Among the truths of faith there are, then, some that do not have to be revealed, but it is good that they have been, and some that must be revealed, because otherwise there would be no way of arriving at them. St. Thomas gives the name "natural theology" to those truths of faith that the human intellect can arrive at on its own, through great effort, discipline, and preparation, in contrast to "supernatural theology," which deals with truths based on revelation This distinction between natural theology and supernatural, or revealed, theology is another important distinction. Natural theology is based on philosophical assumptions; supernatural theology, on revealed truths.

Natural theology, knowledge of things divine based solely on philosophical, natural reflection, is an integral and very essential part of the principal philosophical discipline, whicʰ, since ancient times, has been known as the philosophy of being. The object, or subject matter, of this branch of philosophy is that which is, that which exists, be it a tape recorder, a human being, the earth, a flower, or an atom. If something exists, then, by virtue of the very fact that it exists and is something, it is an object of this science. A tape recorder as a tape recorder will be an object of technology; the planet earth as the planet earth can be an object of astronomy or geography; a human being can be an object of anthropology or some other science, such as medicine. But if we consider each of these objects from the aspect of its existence, as something that is, then we are engaged in the philosophy of being—the wonderful, difficult, controversial science of metaphysics.

The name "metaphysics" arose for purely bibliothecal reasons and refers to that which goes beyond the physical, the province of the particular sciences (*meta* in Greek means "beyond"). Natural theology is the core, the main part, of metaphysics. Consequently, genuine metaphysical thought is basically theological thought. Genuine metaphysics is in some sense theology because, in analyzing everything from the aspect of its existence, metaphysics necessarily extends to the ultimate reason of this existence—God.

Here we are already touching upon the realm that constitutes the quintessence of philosophical thought, especially St. Thomas' thought. Philosophy has developed in such a way that it encompasses a whole series of disciplines: ethics, aesthetics, philosophical anthropology, etc. Their root, their source, their fundamental point of departure and point of arrival is the philosophy of being, or metaphysics.

Here, too, we encounter the question of whether there can be a "Christian philosophy." Strictly speaking, there is no such thing as a Christian philosophy, since philosophy exists outside of and prior to faith. Here there is neither believer nor unbeliever, Christian nor Muslim—just people who philosophize. On the other hand, it is a historical fact that philosophy is engaged in by Christians. In that case, philosophical reflection becomes Christian philosophy, but in a different sense from the one considered above. For philosophy to be philosophy, it cannot contain any premises or assumptions that are truths of faith.

Thomists often encounter the charge that St. Thomas based his philosophy on revelation. Nothing could be further from the truth. Not one of his philosophical conclusions is derived from revelation. Certain philosophical questions may arise as a result of reflecting upon the truths of faith, but that is an entirely different matter. For example, the philosophical question concerning existence has its source in theological reflections on God as Creator; it might never have appeared at all were it not for the motivation provided by the notion of creation *ex nihilo*, a purely religious motivation. But this in no way means that philosophy rests on the premises of faith or on assumptions derived from revelation.

St. Thomas repeats to the point of monotony that *auctoritas*—the authority of revelation (the Scriptures) or of some wise person—can never serve as an argument in philosophy; here only rational, intellectual reasons can come into play. In the beautiful treatise *De Veritate*, St. Thomas writes: *Imposibile est quod de eodem sit fides et scientia* (*De Veritate* 14, 9) —it is impossible with respect to the same object to have both knowledge and faith (we should add: simultaneously). Either we know that *A* exists, or that *A* is *B*—or we believe it; the one excludes the other. There are moments when we say with complete conviction, I know that God exists, but there are also other moments when our intellectual edifice starts to fade, and then we only believe: *Credo in unum Deum*. The same truth appears to us at one time as a truth of faith and at another as a truth of knowledge; it cannot be simultaneously an object of faith and of knowledge.

A related issue that arises here concerns the weakness and strength of various kinds of truth. Faith is the weakest form of truth in terms of certitude—the weakest, for example, in relation to the certitude of mathematical truth, which has the greatest certitude. At the same time, however, faith is in another sense the most certain, for as soon as I accept faith I acknowledge that it is based on divine authority. Then, despite all its cognitive frailty, the strength of a truth revealed by faith turns out to be (and this is the amazing paradox!) far more profoundly—though differently—grounded than a mathematical truth. A similar paradox arises with respect to the truths of metaphysics.[8] St. Thomas emphasizes that from a practical point of view faith is necessary, that the world would be a dark and dismal place were it not for revelation, since only a very few arrive at metaphysics and at a metaphysical knowledge of God.

In the prescientific philosophizing accessible to all, there is always, of course, some consciousness of the Absolute at the basis of our philosophical reflections. But in order to be so certain of God's existence that we could say, I know that God exists, our knowledge must be fully conscious and rationally demonstrated, and this requires both simplicity of spirit and intellectual maturity. St. Thomas says that only very few people reach this point and only after a long time: *est a paucis et per longum tempus* (*ST* I, 1, 1). Metaphysics deals with difficult truths, truths that, unlike the truths of mathematics, are beyond the grasp of a young mind. Mathematicians, on the other hand, are often geniuses in their youth.

But why should metaphysics be any different from mathematics in this regard? First of all, metaphysics requires a great deal of experience. One can be a mathematician if one has an exceptional talent for doing calculations, but intellectual prowess alone does not suffice for being a metaphysician; for this one needs many years of experience as well. St. Thomas also says that some people are simply incapable of thinking metaphysically; they find it extremely difficult. Finally, the struggle for survival is sometimes such an all-consuming task that, if there were no revelation, people would simply not find the necessary *otium*, the necessary leisure, for engaging in the kind of reflection needed to arrive at such knowledge.

This brings us to another important point: Christianity is diametrically opposed to Gnosticism. Gnosticism (we shall later return to this topic) was and still is a very dangerous Christian heresy. The great saint Irenaeus, Bishop of Lyons (2nd c.), battled mainly with the Gnostics. One of the central tenets of Gnosticism is the belief that people can be divided up into basically two groups: spiritual and material, pneumatics and somatics (from the Greek words *pneuma*, "spirit," and *soma*, "body"). Only pneumatics are capable of understanding lofty matters, and the rest of humanity, the vast majority of human beings, are ordinary meat-and-potatoes folk, to whom it is not even worth talking about such things.

Christianity has always taken a completely different point of view. St. Thomas, for example, says that everyone is entitled to know the highest metaphysical truths. We may not conceal such truths from anyone, especially when it comes to truths of faith that are also truths of metaphysics. Revelation is given to all precisely because everyone, even the lowliest, ought to have open access to these highest truths. This principle has always been emphasized by thinkers who follow the line of orthodox Christian thought.

We must also bear in mind that, when it comes to ascertaining the existence of God, even the highest knowledge attainable in the natural sciences is inadequate. The natural sciences should, of course, lead to a synthesis that opens the way for addressing the deepest religious issues and theological questions, but metaphysics alone is the proper course, the proper path, that leads to the natural knowledge of God. Only metaphysics, the philosophy of being, allows us to properly assess what exists—and in this sphere every error has serious ramifications. St. Thomas, in what has come to be known as the *Philosophical Summa*, writes: *Nam error circa creaturas redundat in falsam de Deo scientiam et hominum mentes a Deo abducit*—an error about creatures is reflected in a faulty knowledge of God and turns our minds away from God (*Contra Gent.* II, 3, 1). This would seem to be a very serious matter, and those who say philosophy is unnecessary are simply wrong. Philosophy gives us a kind of knowledge about creatures that the natural sciences cannot provide, and it leads us to the eternal reason of all beings, to God.

5

What is Metaphysics?

We now come to a particularly difficult stage of our reflections. It is a threshold we must cross in order to better understand all that is to follow. One of the things that makes it so difficult is that we must now delve into the very heart of philosophy. Do not become discouraged if you have trouble with some of the language or with certain new and unfamiliar concepts.

In discussing the relation of philosophy, and of science in general, to faith, we have already had occasion to refer to metaphysics more than once. Now we will take up the question, What is the essence of philosophy? Or, to put it another way, what is the essence of what we have called philosophical contemplation? In asking this question, we shall also be asking about the essence of metaphysics, for metaphysics is the core, the very heart, the most essential "repository," so to speak, of philosophical thought.

Over the years philosophy has been viewed in a variety of ways, and many different answers have been given to this question. For centuries now, our European culture has been faced with a situation in which there is no clear consensus concerning the nature and value of that which the Greeks called philosophy and which, as philosophy, became part of our whole cultural heritage. Moreover, in more recent times, there has been a deliberate and systematic tendency—which today is very pronounced in certain circles—to distort and disparage the dignity of philosophy in general and of metaphysics in particular.

It is important for us to be aware of this. The younger generation has undoubtedly been exposed to numerous views that regard metaphysics as a synonym for nonsense, as a superstitious, scientifically meaningless preoccupation with unverifiable matters. To pursue metaphysics, it is said, is like conjuring up spirits or "spinning tables." Kant called a metaphysician a ghost-seer (*ein Geisterseher*). Unfortunately, this pernicious and sinister distortion of the meaning of the term metaphysics, this misrepresentation of what philosophy really is in the best and deepest sense of the term, has become commonplace.

This, then, is how the educated public views the matter and how metaphysics has been presented. As a result, scientific philosophy has become restricted to a minimalist type of knowledge. For those who hold this view, philosophy is limited to an investigation of the functioning of the mind and language, to an organization of the concepts with which we operate, and, basically, to a critique of our cognitive powers. European philosophy in recent years has veered away from metaphysical issues in the classical sense of the term. Over the course of time, metaphysics met with increasing disdain and ridicule, and its place at the center of philosophy was taken over by the philosophical discipline known as the theory of knowledge. The proper concern of philosophy was thought to be not reality but our knowledge of reality. This was an extremely important shift, which resulted in philosophy becoming a far less influential force in contemporary European culture and playing a much smaller role in determining the visage of our spiritual culture than in times past, when metaphysics was still at the center of philosophy.

Metaphysics continues to get a bad press; it is not recommended, given the way it is commonly understood today. While it may no longer be viewed as something akin to occult experiences like the conjuring up of spirits, the charge most frequently heard against it is that those who engage in philosophy, and especially those who pursue metaphysics, withdraw from the real world, escape from reality. One often hears the accusation that in St. Thomas' concept of being there is something so far removed from reality that, when we engage in metaphysics, instead of coming to know reality better, we actually detach ourselves from it and escape from it. Consequently, those who pursue metaphysical philosophy would be the opposite of realists; they would be people who, instead of being in touch with real things in the surrounding world, busy themselves with abstractions, with products of the imagination, products of the mind.

This, then, is how philosophy is frequently viewed, and we should admit that we ourselves may often think of philosophy in this way. When we say, without further comment, that metaphysics, the very heart of philosophy, is the philosophy of being, this does not tell us much. If we ask, What is being? we often hear the response that being is nothing but a pure abstraction, for it is neither this nor that; no matter what we look at, this is still not the being we seek. In thinking about this question and the answer to it, we slowly come to the heart of the matter, to an attempt to answer the question, What is being ultimately? What is this reality dealt with in metaphysical philosophy? St. Thomas seems to be the only one who came up with a satisfactory answer to this question. In order to understand his answer, we shall have to carry out something on the order of a philosophical meditation.

Consider any object whatsoever—a plant, an animal, or some product like a table, a chair, etc. When we look at such an object, we can wonder about it and ask, What is it? In answering such a question, we point out what distinguishes that object from all other objects and what most fully characterizes it. That is to say, we point to its essence (*essentia*). We have just come upon a very important philosophical term: essence. Whenever we ask, What is it? What is this? we are always asking about a thing's essence. On the other hand, we focus on something completely different when, in observing or thinking about some object, we ask, Does it exist? Not, What is it?—but simply, Is it? Does that object exist? We are then dealing with an entirely different aspect, an entirely different side, of the object—its existence (*esse*).

We thus arrive at a fundamental distinction in the philosophy of being, the distinction between essence and existence. We have here two sides, two aspects, two faces, as it were, of a thing: its essence (which we also refer to as the thing's nature) and its existence. The latter accentuates the fact that the thing exists, that it is not just a product of someone's dreams, imagination, or desire, but is a really existing object. St. Thomas, it should be noted, is truly the only philosopher who clearly and distinctly articulated the primacy of existence. Existence is in all things incomparably more important than essence.

If in doing philosophy we were to confine ourselves to a consideration of the essential side of things, if we were to deal with their essence from various aspects and ignore the question of their existence, we would then fall into the error known in philosophy as essentialism (from the Latin word *essentia*, "essence"). We can see how easy it would be in such essentialism to depart from reality, to obliterate the boundary between the real world of independently existing beings and the world of imaginary or conceptual beings, beings of the mind, supplied by our inner mental world.

For St. Thomas the essences of even the most excellent things, when stripped of existence, are as nothing in relation to the existence of even the most insignificant thing. A golden mountain or a mountain full of diamonds that does not exist is infinitely less valuable as a being than even the smallest speck of dust or atomic particle, if it really exists. This may seem so banal and obvious that it hardly warrants discussion, but for philosophy it is a fundamental issue. In the whole cadre of philosophers down through the ages, almost no one, and no one as forcefully as St. Thomas, drew attention to this matter and stressed its significance. Philosophers usually forget about this seeming triviality, this fundamental role of existence, and yet what is at stake here is an aspect of reality that is absolutely fundamental in the philosophy of being. St. Thomas not only distinguished essence (*essentia*) from existence (*esse*) in every being, but he also regarded this distinction as real; that is to say, he saw it as truly applying to things, independently of our cognitive operations.

Let us now examine how St. Thomas understands the inner structure of all things, a structure concealed from sensory experience. According to Thomas, everything, whether it be material or spiritual (there are, after all, purely spiritual beings—angels—of whose existence we know on the basis of faith), is made up of two factors. One of these factors is potential (*potentia*). Every tiny newborn child has the potential to grow up to be a fully developed, mature, wise, holy, great human being—or a very evil one. This is potential. In every seed, there exists in a potential way all that will one day develop out of that seed. This potential, says St. Thomas, is not just a concept; it is something very real, a power inhering in things. It is not merely a logical possibility. We should never confuse potential with possibility. Possibility is simply noncontradiction, whereas potential is the real potential to become something that is not yet. In each of us, in everything, whether it be a small child or an elderly person, a tiny seed or a plant, or anything whatsoever in some phase of its spatiotemporal development, in each of these material and spiritual things there is a union of potential and realization. This potential is realized in stages. Realization (*actus*) is the other factor that co-functions and co-exists with potential. *Potentia* and *actus*, as they are called in Latin, and which I will here be calling potential and realization, are the two factors that make up every being.

But, we may ask, did St. Thomas, following in the tradition of Platonic and Aristotelian thought, have to accept the notion that such a composition exists in every being? Yes, he did, because without it (this might seem strange at first) he would not have been able to establish in a convincing way that there really exists a multiplicity of different things, nor would he have been able to demonstrate the essential difference between real things and products of the mind. There once was a view called monistic pantheism (from the Greek *pan*, "all," and *theos*, "god"), which maintained that only one being exists and that all the diverse things around us are simply various manifestations of that one being. In this pantheistic view, the whole world is identified with God, and everything else, all the diversity in this world, is regarded as merely the manifold of the attributes of that one divine being (I shall say more about this view later on). Now, if we want to accept the view that experience forces upon us, namely, that there exists a multiplicity of real and different things, then, according to St. Thomas, we must acknowledge in every being a composition of potential and realization. This is also indispensable for maintaining and understanding the essential difference between real things and products of the mind.

The composition of essence and existence is the most universal of all compositions because it occurs both in material as well as in spiritual beings. Essence performs the role of potential, and existence is its realization. For St. Thomas this composition is neither a hypothesis nor a mental construct but something real, even though we cannot see it. We perceive concrete things with our senses, but we cannot see, experience, or touch their deepest structure; we cannot dissect a thing and place its potential on one side and its realization on another, any more than we can dissect a human being and say: here is the body and here is the soul (we will return to this issue because the distinction between potential and realization will be essential for us when we look at the human being philosophically). This is an inner composition, one that we must presuppose when reflecting on reality, or else we will fall into absurdity. Such is the structure of metaphysical thinking. The theory of potential and realization is not, therefore, a hypothesis in the strict sense of the term; it is not an arbitrary intellectual construct that someone thought up "in an armchair," but an attempt to understand and explain in a profound way what truly resides in reality.

Let us turn now to a few texts from St. Thomas. These texts are beautiful in their Latin rendition. I will try to present them in more ordinary and understandable language. Thomas—contrary to the commonly accepted philosophical view of his day—says that the most valuable aspect of a thing is not its essence, or nature, however complex, rich, and elaborate this may be, but the most excellent factor in everything is its existence: *Esse est actualitas omnium actuum et propter hoc est perfectio omnium perfectionum* (*De Potentia* VII, 2, 9). This passage is untranslatable in its succinctness. What it means is this: existence (*esse*—this term in St. Thomas should always be translated as "existence") is the realization of all realizations (*actualitas omnium actuum*). I said earlier that existence was the realization of potential; potential is realized by existence. Hence, existence is the perfection of all perfections (*esse... est perfectio omnium perfectionum*). In other words, whatever is perfect, whatever is brought to completion and fulfillment in anything, is so thanks to existence.

Most great Christian thinkers, it is worth noting, completely ignored this side of reality. A later great medieval philosopher and theologian, who was a kind of "rival" of St. Thomas, the Franciscan Duns Scotus, treated existence as one of the last and least important attributes in a being. St. Thomas, in contrast, says in the *Summa Theologiae* (I, 8, 1): *Esse autem est illud quod est magis intimum cuilibet et quod profundius omnibus inest cum sit formale respectu omnium quae in re sunt.* The second part of this sentence is difficult to translate, but the first part is very important: *Esse autem est illud*—existence is that which is *intimum cuilibet, magis intimum*—most profound, innermost, deepest. For St. Thomas, it is through existence that each thing comes in contact with God; existence is that which connects both the smallest speck of dust and the greatest, most perfect being with God. Consequently, existence is that which in each thing, as St. Thomas says, *est magis intimum et profundius omnibus*, is deepest of all, that which adorns, consummates, and enriches a thing's nature. All of the attributes of essence are external in relation to this deepest root of all, existence.

The second part of the sentence—*cum esse sit formale respectu omnium quae in re sunt*—is difficult because it requires a full understanding of what was meant in the philosophical and theological language of Thomas' day by the term *formale*, "form." Form, in the Scholastic language of that time, meant that which expresses a given thing most fully and profoundly, that which is, as it were, an expression of its most essential content. Existence is, then, that which is the fullest exponent of a given thing. We should bear in mind that whatever exists is always concrete and particular: it is some concrete, particular thing. There is no such thing as "a human being in general" or "a horse in general"; only particular human beings and particular horses exist, and likewise particular flowers, etc. When in our philosophy we accentuate the aspect of existence in beings, then that philosophy becomes—contrary to what some think of metaphysics—a philosophy of the concrete, a philosophy of the most concrete things; its object is the concrete, that which really exists, and not some abstraction. We need abstraction in order to understand many things, for without the process of abstraction we could not philosophize at all. Nevertheless, philosophy deals with concrete things, and abstraction is only a method.

These issues are frequently confused in existentialism, a contemporary philosophical movement that still enjoys a good deal of popularity today. The source of this confusion lies in the fact that, in later Latin, "existence" is sometimes called *existentia* rather than *esse*, which was St. Thomas' word for it. Although *existentia* is simply another word for "existence," the term as used by existentialists means something completely different from what St. Thomas meant by *esse*. Thomas used the term *esse*—"existence"—to denote the most essential constitutive element of being, whereas existentialists use the term "existence" to refer to the human condition, which is, of course, an entirely different matter. Existentialism is a philosophy about the human being, a philosophical anthropology; it is concerned with the problem of the tragedy, the difficulty, and the grandeur of the human condition, and thus with entirely different aspects of reality from those of interest to metaphysics. Jacques Maritain was right, therefore, when he said in Rome in 1947: *In the strictest sense of the term, St. Thomas is an existentialist, although he is an existentialist in an entirely different sense from contemporary existentialists.*

Existence cannot be grasped in a concept. Why this is so will become clearer when we take up the question of the human being. We can apprehend only the essence, or nature, of a thing conceptually; we express what a thing is in concepts. When, on the other hand, we affirm the existence of a thing, we affirm it either by virtue of sensory experience (we simply see or feel that something exists; we come in contact with it) or in an existential judgment (we say of an object: *A* is—it exists). This is important, for it often happens that philosophers are interested only in what can be grasped in a concept, and, since existence eludes conceptual apprehension, it cannot be an object of philosophical reflection for them. This is certainly not the case with St. Thomas. Existence plays a pivotal role in his philosophy as a whole and especially in his metaphysics. What we already know of Thomas' philosophy of being will allow us now to proceed to a problem that was of fundamental concern to him and that results from his basic assumptions, with which we are already familiar. One could say that this problem is the reason for the whole of his philosophy and theology. It is the problem of God as self-subsistent existence.

6

God as Self-Subsistent Existence

When we observe the things around us, we notice, of course, that they exist. When we reflect upon them more deeply, however, we cannot help but also notice that the existence of each of these things—whether it be the objects that surround us, our planet, or the whole universe, including ourselves—is an unnecessary existence. None of them has to exist. While this may in one sense be difficult for us to accept, in another sense it is extremely simple. All it takes is a moment of deeper reflection to see that none of these things have the sort of nature that would require them to exist. Mathematical beings "must" exist, but they exist in another, very special way. A square must exist because it is a square. An essential necessity prevails in the mathematical world, but the mathematical world is a completely different world from the world of really existing things perceived by the senses. None of these really existing things has to exist, because, as St. Thomas says, the essence of each of these things differs from its existence. We have here a real difference. These things merely participate in existence; it does not belong to their very nature to exist.

These two observations—that what populates reality truly exists and that the existence of all of these beings is unnecessary and contingent (*esse contingens*)—lead directly to the conclusion that there must exist something that is the source of the partial existence of contingently existing things. There must exist something that of its very nature is existence, an existence that is self-subsistent and necessary and in which there is no difference between essence and existence, since the essence of this something is existence (*essentia = esse*). Those familiar with the Scriptures may find in them a distinct echo of all these remarks, but for now we want to stick to pure philosophy. This source of all existence, which must be a necessary existence in order to impart unnecessary existence, which must be a self-subsistent existence in order to impart non-self-subsistent existence, which must be, in short, an existence identical with essence, St. Thomas calls God. He says: this is precisely God, the source of all existence, the source of all contingently (tenuously, partially, minimally) existing things. When we consider different aspects of our surrounding reality

—St. Thomas mentions five such aspects—we come to realize that there must exist an "existence source," so to speak, of all things that comprise the world and of the world itself.

These five aspects are the famous *quinque viae*—the five ways—of St. Thomas, often inaccurately referred to as the five proofs for the existence of God. The term "proof" is misleading, since these ways are far from proofs in today's sense of the term. They are neither mathematical proofs nor the type of proofs found in the physical sciences, nor are they even proofs in the logical sense, although they have a definite logical structure. The logical validity of these inquiries of St. Thomas has been meticulously examined—but that is not the essential point. These reflections, to use Maritain's terminology, are "ways" of approach, which is why St. Thomas does not call them *rationes*, since the Scholastic term *ratio* is equivalent to "proof," but calls them *viae*, "ways." These are, then, five ways in which we approach reality, and, at the end of each of these ways, the same reality appears to us differently, in a different light and hue.

St. Thomas maintains that God's existence is not self-evident to us. He argues against those who think that the statement "God exists" expresses a self-evident truth. A self-evident truth is one we can discover empirically, one we can experience. God's existence is directly evident only to those who have a personal mystical experience of it. Furthermore, a self-evident truth is one that can be communicated to another, but mystical experience is by nature incommunicable and has nothing in common with sensory or logical self-evidence. And so, says St. Thomas, the existence of God is not self-evident in this sense.

On the other hand, our minds would have to be in some way deformed and limited if, after engaging in honest philosophical reflection based on the metaphysical distinctions mentioned above, we thought it were impossible to discover God as the source of all reality. Each of our deeper reflections on the world as existing always does and should lead us to a discovery of God. Here the term *revelabile* again comes to mind, as well as St. Paul's assertion that, by observing the things of this world, we can arrive at a knowledge of God and things divine (see Rom. 1:20).

The five ways all follow the same pattern and all issue in the same result: God appears in each of them as the source of the unnecessary existence we find in every observable being, and thus as a necessarily existing being. Let us now consider the various aspects St. Thomas examines to arrive at this truth.

1. The first way, from motion (*ex motu*), proceeds from the observation of motion and change in the world around us—every change, change in the broadest sense of the term. All change involves development, that is, a passage from potential to realization. Reflection on any change leads us to the simple conclusion that, in order for these various passages from potential to realization to take place, there must exist a being that is fully realized, one that makes this passage from ontically incomplete states to more complete states possible. In Latin realization is called *actus*, and so God is called "Pure Act," a being in whom there is no potential, only realization. We may be tempted here to think that God is, therefore, a static being, a being in whom there is no motion. This is a very typical "human" way of looking at matters pertaining to God. In our world, it may seem as though perfection is synonymous with constant change. In God, however, there is both a fullness of life—as we shall see when we consider the divine attributes—and a complete fullness of realizations.

2. The second way, from the existence of efficient causes (*ex ratione causae efficientis*), asks us to consider reality under the aspect of causality. The whole world, everything that surrounds us, is a play of causes and effects. Everywhere and in everything efficient causes are constantly at work. Efficient causes impart existence; they are transmitters of existence. As a result of some stimulus, something that did not exist is realized. And so, again, in order for all of these secondary causes we observe to be able to operate, there must be a first efficient cause, one that imparts energy and power to all the other causes, yet neither destroying them nor diminishing their worth. This is precisely the *causa omnium causarum*, the cause of all causes.

3. The third way, from the existence of unnecessary things (*ex possibili et necessario*), considers the aspect of reality closest to that which we discussed when speaking of metaphysics as the philosophy of really existing being. The third way invites us to adopt a point of view that allows us to discover the contingency of things, to recognize that whatever we observe is precarious as far as its existence is concerned. These things do not have to exist, they are contingent, and yet they exist. Everything is, so to speak, suspended in "non-independentness;" everything is dependent on a necessary being. God appears here as the necessary being that is the reason for all contingent beings.

4. The fourth way is from degrees of perfection (*ex gradibus perfectionis*). If we look at the things in the world around us, we see that in the

essential order they certainly appear to differ greatly in perfection. Spiritual beings are more perfect than material beings, and, among material beings, the more complex are more perfect than the less complex. These varying degrees of perfection have their basis in a being that, as the fullness of existence, includes all degrees of perfection.

There is a beautiful passage on this topic in St. Thomas' *Commentary on the Prologue to the Gospel of St. John*. (We should remember that St. Thomas was also a diligent commentator on the Scriptures. This is an aspect of his productivity that often goes unnoticed. There is a tendency to think of him only as a speculative philosopher and theologian, but he was also a distinguished biblical scholar, and his commentaries on the Scriptures are an important part of his productivity.) St. Thomas writes: *Cum ergo omnia quae sunt, participent esse, et sunt per participationem entia, necesse est esse aliquid in cacumine omnium rerum, quod sit ipsum esse per suam essentiam, id est quod sua essentia sit suum esse, et hoc est Deus... a quo omnia quae sunt, participent esse*—since everything that exists (*omnia quae sunt*) participates in existence (*participent esse*), and does not have existence of itself, for then it would have to exist, or it would be so perfect that it would give itself existence, therefore, all such things are beings by participation (*entia per participationem*) and not self-subsistent beings. St. Thomas here contrasts a self-subsistent being with a being by participation, one that exists because it participates in existence. It is, therefore, necessary for something to exist at the summit of all things (*in cacumine omnium rerum*), which, through its own essence, would be existence itself (*quod sit ipsum esse per suam essentiam*); in other words, its essence would be its existence.

We have arrived here at a very fundamental truth. St. Thomas reveals to us little by little that there is one and only one being (there cannot be two!) that, in contrast to all other really existing beings, is a being whose essence, or nature, is existence. There is no difference in this being between its essence and its existence. God alone is this being in which the difference between essence and existence, a difference found in all created beings, is obliterated. Here we are at the heart of St. Thomas' theology. An understanding of and meditation upon these teachings will suffice to understand the whole of St. Thomas' philosophy and theology. To understand these things well is to have the key to the whole of St. Thomas' thought. St. Thomas says, very simply: And this is God—*Et hoc est Deus* —this, from which all other existing things derive their existence. God is the only being in which the union of potential and realization, the composition of essence and existence, disappears. This composition is not needed here because God is existence itself.

5. The fifth way is from order and purpose in the world (*ex gubernatione rerum*). This last way considers a fifth aspect, the aspect of order in the world. Not only do beings differ in perfection, but they are also arranged hierarchically. Aristotle said: *The world is not a poorly written tragedy; these are not chaotic fragments, but a harmonious whole.* This thought of Aristotle is very beautiful. Order exists, and it also has its reason, its source; it is a reflection of that in which there is order in the highest degree, namely, God, Pure Act, which is *ipsum esse subsistens*, self-subsistent existence. Such is the result of St. Thomas' philosophical reflection.

Thus, the "ways" lead by different paths to the conclusion that there must be a being whose essence is its existence, a being that is the source of all that exists in an imperfect way. This philosophical reflection coincides with the teachings contained in revelation.

St. Thomas was convinced that the Tetragrammaton, Yahweh, the holy name of God proclaimed to Moses in the Old Testament, should be understood as *the One who is*. Here was proclaimed, said St. Thomas, the name of God that God wished to reveal to humanity: *If the children of Israel ask you who sent you, say, the One who is* (see Exod. 3:14). However these words might be interpreted philologically, it is certain that the idea of existence is somehow contained in them. We find such utterances not only in the Book of Exodus but also in the New Testament, in passages that for us Christians are even more striking. When, for example, Jesus was speaking in the synagogue and, to the words, *You are not yet fifty years old. How can you have seen Abraham?* he replied, *I tell you truly, before Abraham was born, I am* (see John 8:57–58), the Jews were well aware, according to Thomas' interpretation, that the expression *I am* meant that Jesus was the One whose nature it is to exist. *I am* points to the essence of the divine nature.

It is rather surprising that, despite the many commentaries on the Scriptures produced by the Fathers of the Church, this interpretation did not appear until it was enunciated by St. Thomas. When, for example, St. Augustine was reflecting on the passion, he analyzed this passage from the Book of Exodus and gave it an entirely different explanation. He said that *the One who is* means *the One who endures, who does not change*. St. Augustine did not see the aspect of existence as a basic, constitutive element of being; he simply said, *the One who endures, who is unchanging*. In Plato, God is also that which does not change. When Meister Eckhart, one of the great Dominican mystics, analyzed this passage, he interpreted it beautifully but also in an entirely different way from St. Thomas. Eckhart said that when you meet someone in the dark and ask, Who are you? and the person responds, *I am; that is who I am*, this means that the person does not want to reveal his or her name. The person discloses himself or herself as a great mystery: *I am; that is who I am*—that is the end of it; one ought not inquire further.

Only St. Thomas interprets these words in such a way that revelation here coincides with the very core of metaphysical reflection. This is, then, a typical *revelabile*, a truth that has been revealed but that can also be arrived at through philosophical effort, just as we have attempted to reach, by means of philosophical reflection alone, an understanding of what it means to say that God is self-subsistent existence.

St. Thomas, in one of his earliest works, the *Commentary on the Sentences* (the content of which he later occasionally revised, with the *Summa Theologiae* being the final expression of his thought), writes: *In Deo autem ipsum esse suum est sua quidditas; et ideo nomen quod sumitur ab esse proprie nominat ipsum, et est proprium nomen eius*—in God existence and nature are one, and so the name that derives from existence names God in a proper way and is God's proper name (*In 1 Sent.* 8, 1). *Quidditas* refers to a nature as definable, and, says St. Thomas, God revealed God's own proper name to Moses in order to show by way of revelation that God is existence itself.

Gilson notes that St. Thomas, who is usually so reserved when it comes to expressing his emotions, in this one instance, in the *Philosophical Summa* (*Contra Gent.* I, 22), goes into ecstasy over this convergence of philosophy and revelation. Referring to the conclusion that God is *ipsum esse subsistens*, Thomas calls this extraordinary expression of the harmony of revelation and metaphysics *haec sublimis veritas*—this wonderfully sublime truth. It conveys to us the *proprium nomen Dei*, the proper name of God, that inexpressible Tetragrammaton. This name throws light on the very essence of the divine nature. And so the truth that God is self-subsistent existence is a philosophical truth, one we discover by way of natural philosophical reflection—and it is also a truth that God has revealed about God's own self in the burning bush, one we know from the Book of Exodus.

There are those, including even some who hold lofty positions in the hierarchy of the church and in theology, who say that St. Thomas' so-called "proofs for the existence of God" have nothing to offer us today, that they should be expunged from our ministry and catechesis, that they are historical relics no longer needed in this day and age. There is obviously a misunderstanding here. It is not a question of rationalizing, of introducing certain Scholastic subtleties into our thinking, but simply a matter of plumbing the depths instead of remaining on the surface and dealing only with what people find easy and appealing.

Philosophy, of course, does not convert people. It is not a method for achieving direct pastoral results. But if those who are engaged in ministry of one kind or another do not have an opportunity to steep themselves in the highest achievements of philosophical and theological reflection, they ultimately will not have the material, the content, that they should then, in their own words and in a different fashion, communicate to others. The point is not, therefore, to preach these five ways directly from the pulpit or to teach them in religion classes, but rather for each of us to reflect upon and understand these issues as far as we are able. The question of God—the question of God's knowableness, God's nature, and God's profound relation to created things—belongs to the issues that should be most deeply explored and experienced by all responsible and involved believers.

7

The Mysterious Essence of God

The composition of all things from potential and realization, a composition that in its most universal form appears as a composition of essence and existence, leads directly to the cause of existence; that is to say, contingent existence leads directly to necessary, self-subsistent existence, and we call this self-subsistent existence God. *I am; that is who I am* is, as St. Thomas says, the proper name of God. Is there anything else we can know about God by means of natural reflection beyond the fact that God exists and that in God essence and existence are one? Can we know anything about God's essence and attributes?

This issue raises the methodological question of how we arrive at philosophical and theological knowledge of God. Every science concerned with God, every way of knowing God, is called theology. There are, as we know, two kinds of theology: supernatural theology, which is based on revelation, and philosophical theology, which constitutes the essence of metaphysics. The question before us, then, is whether this philosophical theology, this philosophical reflection on God, progresses by way of positive assertions about God, such as "God is *A*," "God is *B*," etc., or whether it develops and advances instead by way of negative assertions, such as "God is not *A*," "God is not *B*," etc. The former approach is called positive theology, and the latter negative theology.

According to common opinion, the Thomistic theology based on St. Thomas' thought is primarily a positive theology that presents a series of affirmative statements about God. This is an illusion. The theology developed by St. Thomas is actually much closer to a negative knowledge of God, a knowledge of God by way of negation, by way of negating rather than affirming. The notion that Thomistic theology is far more positive than negative is a distortion of the actual position of St. Thomas, who places a distinct emphasis upon the mysteriousness not only of God but of reality as a whole. Everything that surrounds us is permeated with mystery, and God is more mysterious still. God is the mystery of all mysteries.

We have already seen that existence is given to us cognitively, but we are also aware that the very fact of existence is an amazing mystery.

There are many things with which we are more or less familiar, but when we take a closer look at them we come to realize that we are surrounded by mystery on every side; we are enveloped by mysteriousness. Only through many veils can we view the reality surrounding us. We are particularly conscious of this in the case of God. In the Book of Exodus we read that death awaits anyone who would look upon the face of God (see Exod. 28:43, 30:21, and 33:20). To gaze directly upon God is so far beyond our human powers that to do so we would have to die, for we would have to leave the order in which we find ourselves if we were privileged to behold that divine face.

The great pagan philosophers of antiquity clearly recognized that the real meaning of all that surrounds us is hidden from our view. Plato, in the famous myth of the Allegory of the Cave, said that all we see are shadows. We are like prisoners chained to seats in a dark cave. We are facing not the mouth of the cave but the opposite wall. Behind us there is a fire burning, and different figures are passing by, casting their shadows on the wall before us. According to Plato, this is the only way we know reality; we see merely the shadows of what truly exists. In a similar vein, Aristotle, a student of Plato, said that the human intellect, wonderful and amazing though it is, is like the eye of a night bird that can see only in the dark, for the light of the sun completely blinds it. We are surrounded by darkness, and we cannot perceive the real essence of things, the light beyond this darkness.

Against this background St. Thomas' doctrine of the analogy of being and the analogical nature of knowledge (analogy means likeness or similarity) becomes more intelligible and instructive. Here we are primarily concerned with the analogy of existence. Between the existence of something in our surrounding world and God's existence there is only a likeness, an analogy. Divine existence is an existence in itself; it has its justification and reason in itself. The existence of everything else is an existence by participation (Lat. *participare*, "to participate in," "to share in"). With respect to both existence and essence, there is only a distant analogy between the things of this world and God.

To say that some object *A* is analogical to another object *B* means that between *A* and *B* there is some sort of minimal identity; some single point, some single element, is the same in both objects, and all their other aspects are different. If, therefore, we say that there is an analogy between the existence of the things in our surrounding world and the existence of God, and also between the essences of these things and the essence of God, we are saying that there are only certain tiny similarities, or minuscule points of contact, so to speak, between these realities, and beyond these similarities lies a whole sea, a whole abyss, of differences. This alone already suggests the mysteriousness of the divine order. But even in the natural order, with respect to all the objects we perceive with our senses, we know how much there is that remains cognitively inaccessible to us. With regard to the things around us, and especially with regard to God and things divine, there is far more that we do not know than we know. A consciousness of mystery is one of the hallmarks of the whole of St. Thomas' theological and philosophical thought.

St. Thomas paraphrased and to a certain extent transformed the opening line of Aristotle's *Metaphysics*. Aristotle wrote that all humans by nature desire to know. This is something so natural for us that without this tendency toward knowledge and the desire to realize it we would not even be human. St. Thomas went even further in his *Summa Contra Gentiles* (III, 57, 4). He wrote: *Omnis intellectus naturaliter desiderat divinae substantiae visionem*—every intellect, human or angelic, every intellectual cognitive power, by nature desires a vision of the divine nature (the word *substantia* here refers to the divine nature). This natural tendency exists in each of us, whether we are aware of it or not.

Here, however, we run up against an obstacle. Whenever we come to know of something, we wish to state more precisely what that something is. In logic this is called defining. We cannot, however, define God in this way. We know only—and this is important to remember—that there exists a supremely perfect being whose essence is existence. This brings us back to something mentioned earlier: we cannot define this essence because existence cannot be grasped in a concept, and we can only define that of which we have a concept, e.g., a fruit tree, an apple tree, a plant. When it comes to existence, however, we have no concept of it. We merely discover or deduce that something exists—in this case, that something is a self-subsistent existence.

Precisely because we cannot define God, precisely because we cannot form a concept of God in the strict sense, we can know better what God is not than what God is. This is why we are condemned to the darkness, to the night, like those cave dwellers in Plato's myth. At the same time, however, we can be certain that at the bottom of this darkness, at its ground, lies a reality that is a self-subsistent existence—God.

Let us return again to history. There was an author by the name of
Pseudo-Dionysius the Areopagite who enjoyed great popularity throughout the medieval period, although his philosophical approach to these
issues was very different from St. Thomas'. Being a Neoplatonist,
Pseudo-Dionysius did not consider the question of existence at all. He is
called "pseudo" because it was later discovered that works originally
attributed to Dionysius the Areopagite were not written by him. In the
Middle Ages, these works were held in high regard, since they had supposedly come from the Dionysius who was converted by St. Paul in the
Areopagus of the Bishop of Athens, and so they were thought to be as
close to the source—as close to Jesus—as the Epistles or the Gospel
itself. Well, this Pseudo-Dionysius (of whom, incidentally, St. Thomas
also made use, interpreting him in his own manner) strongly emphasized
the negative character of theology. He maintained that theology should
mainly compile negative assertions of the type: God is not this, or that, or
some other thing. According to Pseudo-Dionysius, by using such a method
of negative theological reflection we gradually come to an awareness of
what God is.

After St. Thomas, the significance of mystery in theology was stressed
by the great 15th-century thinker Nicholas of Cusa. He wrote a splendid
work for Benedictine novices. It was a difficult work with a very pro-
vocative title: *De Docta Ignorantia (On Learned Ignorance)*. We draw
near to God, said the Cusian, only when, in a learned way, we become
aware that we are not capable of having clear and direct knowledge of
God. "Learned ignorance" is a paraphrase of words thought to have been
uttered by Socrates in ancient times: "I know only that I do not know
anything." We are not speaking here of skepticism or deliberate ignorance.
We are not saying, "I can't know anything about God," but rather, "I
can't know about God in the way that it apparently seems to me that I
know." It is an awareness that I stand here before a mystery. We hardly
need mention how much in this is similar to St. John of the Cross. The
whole "dark night of the senses" and "dark night of the soul" in St. John
is, after all, woven from these same threads in the realm of the mystical
life.

St. Thomas' remarks on this subject are very explicit. This is what he
says in *Quaestio Disputata De Potentia Dei* (7, 2, ad 1): *Est idem esse
Dei quod et substantia, et sicut eius substantia est ignota, ita et esse—*
God's existence is the same as God's nature, or substance (the word

"substance" here means "nature," "essence"). God's essence and existence are identical (we should always keep this fundamental premise in mind). And just as God's essence is unknown to us, so, too, is God's existence: *sicut eius substantia est ignota, ita et esse.* St. Thomas later goes on to say (*De Potentia* 7, 2, ad 11): *Quid est Deus nescimus*—we do not know what God is. We know that God is, that there is a self-subsistent existence, but what it means to be a self-subsistent existence is something we will know only when we have a vision of God. In the *Summa Contra Gentiles* (III, 34, 9), St. Thomas says: *Quid vero sit Deus penitus manet ignotum.* Commenting on this passage, Gilson writes that it would be hard to say of anything that it is more unknown than this, for St. Thomas says: What God is, is completely unknown to us—*penitus manet ignotum.*

These passages very clearly express that we cannot have a positive knowledge of the divine essence. We cannot know what constitutes the essence of the existence that is God's nature because we have no experience of it. In mystical experience, one may get a foretaste of this, but one would not be able to communicate it to another; it would remain one's mystical experience, but it would not be communicable. Here, however, we are concerned with philosophical truths that should be communicated to all.

"Learned ignorance" applies in some measure, therefore, to our relationship to the whole of reality, but it applies most of all to our relationship to the very core of reality, to God. Of course, faith and revelation do give us a certain insight into this mystery of all mysteries. This is especially true in the case of the Trinity. St. Thomas says that philosophy can tell us nothing of the Trinity. St. Augustine, on the other hand, took a different view of the matter. He did not recognize any sharp boundary between philosophy and faith, and he thought that philosophical reflection could somehow lead us to supernatural truths. He wrote fifteen volumes on the Trinity, and in them he attempted to use certain philosophical concepts to facilitate an understanding of the mystery of the Trinity. For St. Thomas, however, it is clear that we know of the Trinity only from revelation. Faith gives us truths that transcend our comprehension. The dogma of the Trinity reveals to us that in God multiplicity and diversity combine with absolute unity and simplicity, but this truth of faith transcends our ability to comprehend it. Likewise, we are incapable of understanding how in God complete perfection and immutability unite with the full dynamism of life. What all of this exactly means, we do not know. Philosophy is silent here; only the perspectives of faith and mysticism bring this mystery to light.

Extreme proponents of faith in one God usually have the most trouble when it comes to the dogma of the Trinity. Their difficulties stem primarily from an anthropomorphic conception of God, from conceiving of God according to a human model. When we say that God is a person, or that God is personal, we should remember that this is to be understood in the sense that the human person to whom we are comparing the divine person is in some way a very weak reflection of what constitutes the essence of the full divine personality. Only analogical knowledge can be of assistance here. We cannot say that God is a person in the same way that a human being is a person. A failure to abide by this kind of analogy in conceiving of God is what leads to those difficulties with the dogma of the Trinity encountered by extreme proponents of faith in one God.

With all the reservations we have made here, with full consciousness of the mysteriousness of God and of the need to rely on analogical knowledge and predication in this realm, and with full understanding that existence is something that escapes our conceptual grasp, the question nevertheless arises, can we really know nothing of the nature of God?

St. Thomas says very clearly: *Impossibile est igitur aliquid de Deo et rebus aliis univoce dici (Contra Gent.* I 32, 7)—it is impossible to predicate something of God and of things in a univocal way, that is, in a way that is not analogical. In some sense, however, we can know these invisible things, these mysterious attributes or properties of God, through a knowledge of the "perfections"—the different features or attributes—of creatures. Let us once again recall St. Paul's famous saying that not only can we know that God is, but we can even infer something more about God and God's essence from an observation of the world (see Rom. 1:20). When we say, for example, that God is good, true, living, and so on, we should remember that we are always proceeding from properties that we find in creatures in a limited form to the very fullness and source of these properties—and that whenever we express this we find ourselves stammering. Our predication of divine attributes cannot help but be a stammer. It can never be an exact expression and description of the reality. This is why the mystics recommend silence far more than positive pronouncements. We return once again to the point that the negative way, characterized by ecstasy, negation, and silence, is here the most certain and proper approach.

Of course, different models, different images, so to speak, may be of help to us in forming some notion of the attributes and nature of God. Nicholas of Cusa, for example, thought that mathematics could be of great assistance to us in this regard: geometric models could lessen the inaccessibility of the divine nature. Since infinity is one of the most essential attributes of God, all the values we find in a finite degree dispersed among creatures come together and become one in God. In God these attributes taken to infinity become identical with one another, just as a triangle with an infinitely long side converges into a straight line. Mathematics tells us nothing of God's existence. Rather, mathematical models are merely one of the ways that facilitate our understanding of the incomprehensible simplicity of God combined with the equally incomprehensible richness of attributes belonging to God. In a similar vein, St. Bonaventure, the greatest Franciscan Doctor of the Church, who wrote so beautifully about the world, said that every creature is a mirror. Every creature, even the most insignificant, is, to a greater or lesser degree, in keeping with its perfection, a mirror reflecting the divine perfections. Bonaventure saw the world as a system of such mirrors. We have here a kind of philosophical transcription of St. Francis' view.

All of these methods (Nicholas of Cusa's mathematicism, Bonaventure's exemplarism, etc.) are intended to help us form some cognitive notion of what God is. They do not, however, give us certain knowledge. In this realm only our analogical knowledge, though extremely limited and imperfect, is certain. Thanks to it we can know that at the bottom of the mystery before which we stand lies a reality and not a void. And so when I say that I know that I know nothing, or when a Hindu speaks of nirvana, this is not an avowal of nothingness or an assertion that nothing is there, but merely a way of saying that we are surrounded by a great mystery. In the face of this mysterious yet so very real reality, the "dark night of the senses" and "dark night of the soul" seem to be a far more reliable avenue of approach than even the best mathematical or metaphorical models intended to aid us in this regard. There is no substitute here for the unique role played by mystical experience. In philosophy, on the other hand, analogical thinking and the way of negation are the only route by which we can advance in our attempt to penetrate, however slightly, into the mystery of God's essence.

8

The Attributes of God

Instead of the classical term "act," I have employed the term "realization." Rather than the traditional terms "potency" and "act," I shall be using the terms "potential" and "realization." Essence is potential and existence is realization. God is full realization, pure realization. The classical formulation puts it this way: God is *actus purus*, which means that God is pure realization, complete fulfillment.

Certain conclusions follow from these basic premises. If God is pure realization, then there is no potential in God. By potential here, I am not speaking of God's ability to do one thing or another, but rather of a factor found in every created being. In this sense there is no potential in God. With respect to God's existence, St. Thomas says: *In Deo... non est potentia ad esse* (*Contra Gent.* I, 16, 1)—in God there is no potential to exist; in God *esse* is completely realized. This is also true of all God's attributes. As self-subsistent existence, God must be a maximally perfect being, because *secundum modum quo res habet esse est suus modus in nobilitate* (*Contra Gent.* I, 28, 2)—the nobility, the perfection, of a being corresponds to the way in which that being exists. Since God is pure, self-subsistent, complete existence, God is also, therefore, a supremely perfect being.

St. Thomas as a philosopher was convinced that existence is interchangeable with goodness. This is an important assertion. Everything that exists is good. Everything without exception! And so God, as self-subsistent existence, must be maximally good. God is goodness itself. Plato reverses the order here. In Plato, God is goodness first and foremost. In Thomas, on the other hand, God is goodness because God is existence. Existence is here the reason of goodness. God is also truth, because truth—contrary to the whole of modern European philosophy—is connected far more with things, with existence, than with the knowing human mind. Truth is the conformity of thought to reality, but truth lies in reality, in existence. That is why when Jesus said of himself, *I am the way, the truth, and the life* (John 14:6), he expressed the very quintessence of the divine attributes: the way is goodness, and together with goodness are truth and life. Why is goodness the way? Because the good is that at which all things aim.

St. Thomas derived a whole series of conclusions from these very simple premises. As pure realization, as *actus purus*, God cannot be composite; from this follows the absolute simplicity of God. We return here to a theological difficulty mentioned earlier, namely, the union of absolute simplicity with the multiplicity of persons in the Trinity. God must be perfectly simple. God cannot be really composite because composition occurs only where there is potential and realization, where there is an essence that differs from existence. Now, if God is absolutely simple, then God must be a spirit—and that is just what Jesus told the Samaritan woman: *God is a spirit* (John 4:24). We have here again a *revelabile*, a philosophical truth that is also a revealed truth.

Every material being is composite. A created spirit, as we shall see, is also composite according to St. Thomas, but less composite than a body. God is absolutely simple, and so in God we find the pinnacle of what it means to be a spirit. Whatever we know as simple and spiritual in things is only a distant reflection of the divine. We have already said that the kinds of personalities we find in the world are only a distant reflection of the personality of God. Animals are not persons, but human beings are persons, and we know more or less why we call them persons. Similarly, when we assert the existence of a spiritual element in human beings, we can say that we see here a distant reflection of what is maximally and fully realized in God.

On this basis, we can say that God, in an infinitely intensified way, must possess what constitutes the essence of spirit—and the essence of spiritual life is to know and to love. Therefore, according to St. Thomas, to God belong the three proper and basic attributes mentioned in Christ's statement: *I am the way, the truth, and the life* (John 14:6), which means, I am will (love), knowledge, and life. These are the three fundamental traits of divinity. There is a striking logic and consistency in these observations of St. Thomas. If his simplest and most basic premises are accepted and reflected upon, they necessarily lead to a conclusion that constitutes a commentary on these words of Christ.

God's knowledge must be maximal. In the *Summa Theologiae* (I, 14, 1) we read: *Cum Deus sit in summo immaterialitatis sequitur quod ipse est in summo cognitionis*—because God is the pinnacle (*in summo*) of immateriality, of spiritualness, God is also, therefore, the pinnacle of knowledge. We already mentioned above that for St. Thomas the essence of spiritual life is knowledge and will; hence, the greater the degree of spiritualness, the greater the degree of knowledge. Animals often have a high level of knowledge, but they do not have the kind of spiritual knowledge that humans have (later we shall see the reason for this difference). If, as faith tells us, angels exist, then the knowledge possessed by these spiritual beings must be far more powerful than that of humans. God, who is *in summo immaterialitatis*, is also *in summo cognitionis*—God, who is at the pinnacle of spiritualness, is also at the pinnacle of knowledge. The primary object of knowledge for God is God's own self. Since everything derives from God as self-subsistent existence and efficient cause, God must, therefore, in knowing the divine self, know all things in the deepest sense.

In St. Thomas' day there were certain proponents of Aristotelianism who interpreted Aristotle in a way completely different from Thomas. They reasoned more or less as follows: If God is a spirit (for Aristotle, God as Pure Act must be a spirit), then God knows only what is spiritual, and so God does not know particular, concrete, material things; God cannot be sullied with knowledge of this whole insignificant material morass. These disciples of Aristotle, interpreting him in the spirit of Averroës (a great Arabian philosopher who at that time entered the Latin world as a commentator on Aristotle and who was at variance with the Christian faith on many points), said that God cannot know everything; God's knowledge is limited to genera and species. God knows and watches over the human species, but God does not watch over individual human beings; God watches over animals in general, but God is not interested in particular, individual animals.

St. Thomas, in sharp contrast to Aristotle, regarded existence as the essence of God. He argued that since God is existence and the source of all existences, and since existence is always concrete and particular rather than general, God must know everything that exists, everything that is dependent upon God for its existence, every concrete being, every smallest, most insignificant thing. Everything must be an object of divine knowledge, for God is not only the final cause of the world—as the Averroists also maintained—but is its efficient cause, the source of its existence, as well. Consequently, says Thomas, God must be Providence. Providence does not watch over the world merely in a general way, but watches over all of the smallest events in the world. Everything falls within the purview of God's knowledge and will. Providence is a particular plan as well as an attentiveness to every minutest detail of that plan (we shall return to this issue when we take up the problem of evil).

God knows everything at once. We are touching here upon the dizzy-ingly profound question of time. Eternity is not simply time that has no end; eternity is transtemporality. We should ponder this very deeply, for it contains, I believe, something extremely important, even for our spiritual life. Since God is in transtemporality, God somehow encompasses all time at once within the divine self. Everything that happens over the course of trillions of years is all in God at once, and God sees it all simultaneously. God also knows everything that exists. Whatever has come into being even for the tiniest faction of time is known by God in God as its root and source. There is great consolation, too, in the thought that whoever comes to partake of eternity will rediscover absolutely everything in God. Noth-ing perishes; there are no missing things, no memories forever gone. The words of the Apocalypse will be fulfilled: there will be no tears, no weep-ing, no mourning (see Apoc. 21:4), for whatever is evil is nonbeing and will cease to exist; only what is will remain, and it is imperishable in God.

Thus, God knows everything at once in motionless eternity.

There is no composition in God; God is absolutely simple. From this it follows that God is a spirit. We ourselves are composite. We find this reflected in that fact that for us to know is one thing and to will is another. Knowing arises from a certain dispositional source known as the intellect, and willing is an operation of the will. In us there is a difference between intellect and will. Although it is I who both know and will, I realize that there is a composition in me. In God there is no such composition. God has no faculties, no intellect and will, although in the Old Testament God is often portrayed in a very human way. We see God willing, regretting, feeling, getting angry, refusing, etc. These are all metaphorical represen-tations. God *is* knowledge and will. In the language of philosophy, we say that in God knowledge and will are substantial; they are identical with God. We have already seen that the primary object of God's knowledge is God's own self, and in this divine self God knows all things.

The same holds true of the divine will. God must primarily will and love God's own self, but in this divine self God loves all things. St. Thomas here takes up the beautiful motif of Platonic philosophy that the good is diffu-sive of itself. God, in willing the good, that is, in loving the divine self, wishes to share this self with other beings. This is the ultimate reason for creation, a point to which we shall return when discussing God's relation to the world. God cannot will or love contradictory things, impossible things. Contradictory things—things in which contradictory attributes are combined, such as a square that is simultaneously a circle—cannot be an object of God's will or love. On the other hand, everything that exists, everything without exception, is loved by God because it is willed by God. St. Thomas makes an important point here that should be emphasized: God does not love creatures because they are good, but they exist and are good because God loves them. God's will, God's love, is the cause of the goodness and existence of things.

Here again a new *revelabile* comes to light, a new *sublimis veritas*, as St. Thomas calls it, a marvelous, fascinating new truth: God is identical with truth and love. In these observations of St. Thomas we hear an echo of the words of St. John: *Deus caritas est*—God is love (1 John 4:8). Just as God is truth, so, too, is God love, and this love is the reason for everything that exists. There are no exceptions here: even an evil spirit would not exist were it not an object of God's love. An evil spirit, a rebellious spirit, is morally bad, but as a being it is good and it is an object of divine love, for otherwise it would not exist at all.[9] All beings, without exception, are loved by God. God's love makes them good, both in the order of nature and in the order of grace. In both of these orders, goodness is a result of divine love.

If we consider these three attributes—goodness, truth, and life—then all that can be said of the divine life is actually a consequence of what has already been said. We often have a shallow and superficial understanding of life. We should bear in mind that the fullness of life is not merely the sum of our biological and sensory functions. Rather, life consists above all in the most perfect activity possible of the two functions characteristic of spiritual life—knowing and loving. This is the fullness of life.

St. Augustine attempted to show in his reflections on the Trinity how the life of the Trinity pulsates with knowledge and love. St. Thomas also took up this theme. Activity in these two directions, the realization of knowledge and of love, not with one act following the other but as a single, completely unitary rhythm, takes place in the fullest way possible in God. Consequently, when we say that in God there is complete fulfillment, total realization, this does not mean that in God all is static. Quite the contrary: in God all is supremely dynamic. It is a mystery, however, how this dynamism can be realized not in temporal, successive stages, but as though in a single, unitary, noncomposite burst.

These considerations lead St. Thomas to a very important discovery, namely, that God, in realizing these attributes that are identical with

God's own self, is happy through God's own essence. God is happiness, and God is the sole reason for the happiness of all created things. Thomas writes: *Deus per essentiam suam beatus est quod nulli alii competere potest (Contra Gent.* I, 102, 4)—God is happy through God's own essence, which can be said of no one else. None of us can be happy through our own essence. We can be happy only to the extent that we draw near to God, to happiness itself. God is *per essentiam suam beatus*—God is happy through God's own essence. God, as *the way, the truth, and the life,* is identical with happiness. St. Augustine was right, therefore, when he said in his *Confessions* that if we seek even a fraction of happiness we are really seeking God, even though we may not be aware of it. Even if we were to search for happiness along the most blundering and misguided paths, we would really be seeking God, since every shred of happiness is a reflection of God, whose very essence is happiness. And so even if we were completely unaware of it, even if we happened to be atheists and enemies of God, in seeking happiness we would essentially be seeking God. St. Augustine developed this thought in his *Confessions*.

9

The Relation of God to the World

St. Thomas' philosophy is profoundly theocentric. If we take a proper approach to metaphysical reflection and look at reality from the side of the deepest structure of things, we will find the cause of this structure. Since essence and existence (potential and realization) are the most fundamental constituents of beings, by examining this structure we discover that a self-subsistent existence, a being whose essence is existence, is the cause of the whole of reality. Although this may seem like a very short route, it requires an enormous effort of contemplation, of deep reflection, and not some artificial, abstruse, complicated reasoning that would lead in the end to a conclusion affirming the existence of a self-subsistent cause of the whole of reality—God. We must know how to catch sight of that structure of reality mentioned above.

We turn now from questions dealing directly with God, from what constitutes the very heart of metaphysics, from natural theology, the theology accessible to natural intellectual knowledge, to the problem of God and the world and the relations existing between them. Stripped of ideological tendencies, the contemplation of reality—regardless of whether we focus on some small part of our surrounding world or on the whole of reality, on everything that exists—leads inevitably to God.

In St. Thomas' metaphysics, as we have seen, existence is the deepest aspect of things. And because this existential factor is the deepest aspect of things, God lies at the ground of everything. God encompasses the very depths of all things and permeates them through and through. This must be the case if God is the source, the reason, the ground of existence. This truth is the philosophers' stone for which thinkers yearned, and, at the same time, in it is manifested the God of revelation that appears to us in the words of St. Paul: *In God we live, and move, and have our being* (Acts 17:28). Since everything that exists is good (evils are only privations), everything is permeated to its very core by God, and this is why philosophers, theologians, and mystics could say that God is much closer to us than we realize. The most fundamental thing in us is our existence. God bears this existence within the divine self, and so God is even closer to us than we are to ourselves. These are discoveries to which philosophical reflection directly leads us; we do not need revelation to know them.

In St. Thomas we find a very powerful passage, one that might even shock us with its seemingly pantheistic overtones (*pan* in Greek means "all" and *theos* means "God"; pantheism is the view that everything is God, that God is identical with the world). In the *Commentary on the Sentences*, one of his earliest works, St. Thomas writes: *Deus est esse omnium* (*In 1 Sent.* 8, 1, 2)—God is the existence of everything, but, he adds: *non essentiale sed causale*—not essentially but causally. God is the existence of everything, although God is not existence as a constituent of things but as their efficient cause, as the source from which their existence flows. God is not, therefore, their essential existence, not the existence that unites with essence, since this existence in things is a partial, participatory existence, but their causal existence.

For St. Thomas, as we know, *esse est illud quod est magis intimum cuilibet, et quod profundius omnibus est* (*ST* I, 8, 1)—existence is that factor in us, and in every other object as well, that is deeper than anything else. *Intimum* means innermost, deepest, reaching to the very core. Existence is that which is innermost *et quod profundius omnibus est*—and that which is most profound in every being, in everything. And because God, as we read a moment ago, *est esse omnium*—is the existence that is the cause of the insignificant, partial existences in all things, St. Thomas goes on to say: *oportet quod Deus sit in omnibus rebus et intime*—it is fitting, and even necessary, that God be in all things, *et intime*—and be there in a profound way (*ST* 1, 8, 1).

We are touching here upon the problem of the divine presence. Philosophy itself already opens before us stunning horizons, revealing the abidance of God, as the source of existence, in absolutely everything. God permeates all things. Everything is saturated with God. Yet, since God is not in things as their essential existence but as the cause of their existence, as their causal existence, there is no pantheism here. The totality of things, the world as a whole, is not identical with God, but rather God is that *in which we live, and move, and have our being*. In philosophical language, we call this truth the immanence of God. *Manere* means "to remain," "to abide," and *immanere* means "to abide in." The immanence of God, therefore, signifies that God abides in all things, in everything as a whole and in every particle of this whole.

An extraordinary mystery to which philosophy points, but that it is absolutely incapable of explaining to us, is that God's immanence unites with absolute transcendence. The word "transcendence" comes from the Latin term *transcendere*, "to go beyond." God, who most profoundly abides in things, at the same time infinitely transcends the whole world and everything in it. This is a mystery as incomprehensible as the multiplicity and unity of the Trinity. These are things we supposedly know, things we supposedly hold as truths of faith, but we probably seldom stop to think about them, and seldom under the guidance of such deep philosophical thought to light our way as that provided by St. Thomas. Immanence and transcendence, the one and the other in an identical degree—the *abiding in* and the *going beyond*—properly characterize God's relation to the world only when taken together. "World" here signifies both the sum of all created things, all existing things apart from God, and every particle of this enormous whole.

Let us now consider the various attributes from which the proper names of God are derived.

"The One" signifies that God is absolutely one. Philosophy, and not just revelation, tells us that God as pure realization can be only one. There cannot be two pure realizations, two pure acts. There can be only one pure act. If there were two, then one would differ from the other in some respect, and if it differed in any way whatsoever then it could become the other; it would not be complete realization. There can only be one complete realization, and this is the reason for the unity of God.

"The Immutable" tells us that in God there is no change. God is absolutely unchangeable. We reason here in a similar fashion. Complete realization does not permit of further realization. Every change is a passage from potential to the realization of that potential. Consequently, if in God there were variation, then God would not be pure realization, pure act, and so God must be both absolutely one and unconditionally immutable.

We can also discover that God is both eternal, transcending all temporal change, and infinite, transcending all limits. All of this results from reflecting upon the meaning of complete, pure realization, which in the case of God is self-subsistent existence. We must constantly keep returning to that central point of our discussion where we spoke of God as *ipsum esse subsistens*—self-subsistent existence. This is a fundamental point, without which the matters subsequently discussed would not be fully intelligible.

The topic of the attributes of God occupies a place of its own in the history of theology. There were many famous theologians—not just Christian, but Arabian, Jewish, and Hindu as well—who viewed God through one of the divine attributes. This is not to say that these different ways of viewing God were wrong; the question is simply which of them was most profound.

The great Neoplatonic view, which had its source in Plato and was taken up by St. Augustine and his followers, accentuated the unity of God. Plotinus, the founder of Neoplatonism, called God "the One." Of chief importance to Neoplatonic theologians is that God is one, absolutely uncomposed, and all of God's other attributes seem to result from unity. For St. Augustine, along with unity the attribute that distinguishes God from all other things is absolute immutability. We already mentioned the kind of biblical exegesis St. Augustine gave to the phrase: *the One who is*. He interpreted these words to mean *the one who does not change, who endures*. Thus, absolute immutability would here be the source of all the other divine perfections.

Duns Scotus, one of the greatest Franciscan philosophical theologians, gave primacy to a different attribute of God: infinity. He observed that there is one and only one infinite being, and that being is God. And so Scotus divided the whole of reality into two realms, encompassing the two categories of being: infinite being—God, and finite being—all other things.

A variety of historical conditions induced a great scholar, William of Ockham, founder of a new orientation in late medieval philosophy and theology, to accentuate the freedom and power of God. The proper name of God, according to Ockham, is absolutely omnipotent being.

These are examples of different theologies, different views of what is most important in God. St. Thomas did not deny any of these attributes; he accepted them all, but he saw as the reason for them the fact that God is self-subsistent existence. This for St. Thomas is God's proper name and the proper reason of all the divine attributes, as well as the key to understanding the relation of God to the world.

In thinking about the problem of the creation of the world, we should rid our heads of the naive and false notion that creation is a fact that took place somewhere, once upon a time, millions of years ago and has long since ceased. This is a mistaken understanding of creating and creation. To create is to give existence to what does not exist, and this is constantly going on. Hence, the statement, *conservatio est continua creatio* (*ST* I, 103, 3)—the conservation of things in existence is a continuation of the act of creation, a continual creating—is not a metaphor. It should be taken literally: creation is going on continually. From St. Thomas' perspective, the assertion that the world is created is not only a revealed truth. Here, again, we have a *revelabile*, a revealed truth that we can also attain with our intellect. If we recognize the need for a reason of the existence of things, then the assertion that existence derives from this reason, from this source, is also an acknowledgment of the act of creation. This is precisely what constitutes the essence of God as creator.

The fact of creation as an ongoing occurrence in which we continually live is an important and real aspect of reality. It is quite another matter that, as faith tells us, the world at some point began to exist. This does not mean that the act of creation happened once and for all, and that after creating the world God simply forgot about it. That would be a deistic point of view. St. Thomas presents the matter very differently: God is like—to use a metaphor—a battery from which a constant current of existence flows out to all things. Only God is Creator; there can be no intermediary creating. Although we may sometimes refer to human beings as creators, it is never in the sense in which God is Creator. Only God is Creator, and this creative act proceeds from God alone, because *creatio est quaedam acceptio esse* (*In 2 Sent.* 1, 2, c.). *Creatio* here means to be created, and to be created is to receive existence from the source of existence—from God. God alone is the source of existence for everything without exception, and so God is Creator.

It is important historically, and worth noting, that the philosophical concept of God as Creator was completely unknown to ancient philosophy. The ancient philosophers did not introduce this idea into their inventory of concepts at all because they associated creation with a beginning in time. Since they thought that the world had always existed, the concept of creation did not enter into their reckoning, much less creation from nothing. The world had always existed. They wondered about what the world was made of, what its elements were, what constituted its essence. The question of the reason of the existence of the world arose in philosophy only under the impulse of the religious thematic, the description of the creation of the world presented in the Bible. The revelation contained in the Book of Genesis said that in the beginning there was nothing until God created something, that the world came into being out of nothingness.

St. Thomas also emphasized that the act of creation is for God an absolutely free act. Here St. Thomas seems to reflect the view of a teaching of a later thinker, William of Ockham, who said that the creation of the world is not something necessary. Neoplatonic philosophy saw the world as somehow necessarily emanating or flowing out of its source, the One. St. Thomas' view was altogether different: the world is entirely dependent upon a free act of God. God's external activities (*ad extra*), in contrast to God's inner activity (*ad intra*), are absolutely free activities; there is no necessity in them. Necessity is, in a mysterious way, combined with freedom in the inner life of God, which for us, of course, is incomprehensible. All we can do is call attention to this mystery and this truth.

We should remember that the world need never have existed. If there were no world, that would change absolutely nothing in the most essential life that is the life of the Trinity. The glory of which Christ speaks in the Gospel—*Glorify me in Your presence with the glory that I had with You before the world began* (John 17:5)—is precisely the divine inner life, totally independent of the world. The world is completely contingent; its whole existence is dependent upon a free decision of God.

God knows all beings—not only those that now exist or that at any time existed anywhere in the universe, in all the galaxies and in the entire spiritual world, but also all possible things, i.e., all noncontradictory things (for whatever is contradictory is impossible). And so, speaking of God in human terms, we can say that God has an idea of everything that is, was, will be, or is possible. As St. Thomas says, *Deus intelligit plures rationes propriae plurium rerum quae sunt plures* (*ST* I, 15, 2, c)—God has proper concepts of all things. Because God knows all beings, there are also in God models, so to speak, of all possibilities, of all possible worlds.

St. Thomas points out that the world that exists, the world in which we live, our surrounding world, is not the only possible world; it is one of an infinite number of possible worlds. It is also not the most perfect world, contrary to what Leibniz, a great 18th-century philosopher, thought. Every possible world, including our own real world, must be relatively perfect and relatively imperfect. The world in which we live is not, then, the most perfect world: it is perfect to the extent that God is in some way reflected in it. One of the innumerable models of possible worlds is called into existence by God: in this consists the continual creation of the world, the unceasing *continua creatio*, an act of creation stretching out into time and space. Let us, then, remember that this world in which we live and move could have been totally different and could also have not existed at all, and yet this would not change anything in God or diminish the majesty, fullness, and perfection of God.

In St. Thomas' day the question of the eternity of the world was a hotly debated issue. The ancient philosophers, after all, had maintained that the world had no beginning. St. Thomas' view on this topic is worthy of note; it also throws light on his understanding of the act of creation. The divine creative act, according to Thomas, is not something that once occurred a long time ago, but something that is constantly occurring. That the world began in time, that a specific quantity of segments of time have elapsed from the moment when there was nothing and the world began, is a *credibile*; one can and should believe this, but, according to St. Thomas, it is not a truth that can be philosophically or scientifically proven. Moreover, in view of this, the proposition that the world began in time is a *revelatum* and not a *revelabile*; it is a revealed truth and one that philosophy cannot arrive at on its own.

On the other hand, the thesis that the world is created, that it must be created if its exists, is a *revelabile*, a truth to which we are led by philosophical thinking. Even if we were to believe that the world had always existed, that matter had always existed, St. Thomas would say: it is completely irrelevant whether matter has always existed or whether it had a beginning in time. In either case it is created, because it has no existence in itself. In other words, if we were to accept the hypothesis that the world has always existed, St. Thomas would say that this in no way undermines the fact that it is created. This is an important and timely point in view of our present-day discussions with the Marxists, often especially in student circles. Were it the case that the world, that material beings, had no beginning in time and had always existed, this for St. Thomas would in no way affect the thesis that they are created, for they are dependent in their existence on a creative act of God, on the free will of God, on a self-subsistent existence.

To be created means to receive existence, to exist in an unnecessary way, to have a participatory existence deriving from a self-subsistent existence —that is the essence of being created. God is self-subsistent existence, and so God must be the efficient cause, the giver, of existence. God is also immanent in all things, as their efficient cause, their *esse causale*, and, at the same time, transcendent in relation to all things, since God infinitely surpasses them all and is ontically completely independent of them.

This should help us understand how completely foreign to St. Thomas are such theories as pantheism, the view that God is identical with the world, or deism, the view that God created the world once and for all and then "forgot" about it, that God arrived at the Sabbath and then had nothing more to do with the world. God is not the soul of the world, nor does God stand outside the world. God permeates the world through and through as the ultimate source of being. God is the efficient and final cause of everything that happens in the world. But does this also include evil?

10

The First Cause and Secondary Causes

God's creative activity is very different from ours. There is, of course, a similarity between an artist and a craftsperson. Plato makes use of this motif in the *Timaeus*, where the Demiurge fashions the world out of clay. There is also a certain analogy between God and a potter or sculptor—but precisely here lurks the danger. If this analogy is taken too literally, it suggests the notion of some shapeless material that is somehow equal in duration to the artist using it. With God this is absolutely not the case.

God's creative act is something completely different from artistic creativity; it is the giving of existence to the thing created. A human creator —an artist or a craftsperson—is only the cause of bringing something about, a *causa fiendi*, a cause of becoming, but the Creator is a cause of existence. There is a very fundamental difference between these two kinds of causes. St. Thomas, referring to *causa efficiens*, efficient cause, writes: *Nomen causa importat influxum quemdam ad esse causati* (*Commentary on the Metaphysics* V, 751)—the concept of a cause implies or entails a certain influence on the existence of what is caused, on the existence of the effect of the action of the cause. In efficient causation some sort of existence is always transmitted to the effect by the cause.

If God were to create beings that could exist without a divine act that confers existence upon them, God would create contradictory beings, because God would create "Gods," and the concept of a created God involves a contradiction (see *Contra Gent.* II, 25). But—and this is important—every creature, each in its own sphere, is also an efficient cause. God is not the only efficient cause in the universe. God conserves in existence everything that surrounds us and ourselves as well, and these are all causes in some narrower or broader finite sphere. All created things are secondary causes; God alone is a first cause, the cause of all causes. God, as was mentioned earlier, is closer to us than we are to ourselves. Likewise, *Deus principalius est causa cuiuslibet actionis quam etiam secundae causae agentes* (*Contra Gent.* II, 67, 5)—God is a fuller cause of every action, a cause in a more important and more powerful way, than secondary causal agents. This means that God is more of a cause of the actions of any creature than that creature itself is.

This opens up an enormous field of discussion: How on earth can God possibly be the cause of the evil acts performed by human beings! To this St. Thomas responds: God is the cause of all causes, both necessary and free. God so values freedom—which, as we shall see, is exclusively a property of angels and humans—freedom is such a magnificent thing, that God, as the cause of causes, is also the first cause of free acts in the world of freedom. This universal activity of God, the first efficient cause, causes everything in everything, and yet, even though it is true causation, it does not rule out freedom. This again is a mystery: God is the cause of all causes, both necessary and free, without canceling out necessity or annihilating freedom.

The universal and fundamental activity of the first cause does not, therefore, diminish the authentic activity of creatures. Hardly any other philosophy so strongly supports the autonomy, the independence, of created beings. We are true masters of our actions; animals are really causes of their activities; so, too, are plants, minerals, and atoms. The whole of this causation is, at the same time, somehow sustained and brought about by the ultimate causality of the activity of the divine will.

In this connection, I would like to draw attention to two passages from St. Thomas. The first one is this: *Prima causa ex eminentia bonitatis suae rebus aliis confert non solum quod sint, sed etiam quod causae sint* (*De Veritate* XI, 1)—the first cause, by reason of the eminence of its goodness (*eminentia bonitatis suae*), endows other things not only with their existence but also with their status as causes. Creatures participate in God by virtue of being causes. Not only do they participate in God as self-subsistent existence, but they also participate in God as cause. They reflect, each to a different degree, the ultimate causality of God. The second passage, which stands as a wonderful *credo* of St. Thomas' humanism, can be regarded as an axiom of his thought: *Detrahere actiones proprias rebus est divinae bonitatis derogare* (*Contra Gent.* III, 69, 16) —to deprive things of their proper activities is to disparage divine goodness. This is an important statement. It suggests that the more a creature develops, the more it expresses the perfection of God. In other words, the more a creature realizes its potential, the more fully is the *bonitas Dei*, the goodness of God, revealed in it.

Thomas wants to say that no being can properly tend toward God as its end if it does not fulfill its designated good. This is the principle of the autonomy of the world, a principle that Maritain so strongly emphasized: every being must develop in keeping with the laws governing its nature and must reach a certain level of development, and only then can it fully contribute to the glory of God. St. Thomas says very unequivocally: *Unumquodque tendens in suam perfectionem tendit in divinam similitudinem* (*Contra Gent.* III, 21, 6)—every being that tends toward its own perfection tends toward the divine likeness. This thought of St. Thomas is expressed by Gilson in the following way: *Sauvegarder les droits de la créature, c'est... le seul moyen de sauvegarder les droits de Dieu*[10]— safeguarding the laws of creatures is the only way of safeguarding the laws of God. These are strong words. We may never trample upon the laws of creatures, and the safeguarding, the full development, and the acknowledgment of the laws of creatures, of everything that comes from nature, is the best way of preserving the force of the laws of God.

Against this background, we can also better understand St. Bonaventure's view of the world. Although he derived his thought from other sources and developed it in a different context, on this point his position is close to St. Thomas'. For St. Bonaventure, the whole world is like a great system of mirrors: there are tiny mirrors and gigantic ones, very clear mirrors and rather dim ones, and they are all intended to reflect God, to mirror the divine perfections. St. Thomas emphasizes that this likeness of divine perfection is realized in a perfect way solely and exclusively in the Word, *in Verbo*. Only the Divine Word, who is born, and not created, is a full and perfect reflection of the glory of the Father.

But can a world in which there is so much evil be regarded as a mirror of God? We often hear it asked: Why didn't God create a world in which there was no evil? Philosophy—which must approach every question with a cool head, seek out reasons, and, as far as possible, eliminate emotional bias if it is to think correctly and clearly—must arrive at the following sort of conclusion: Just as God cannot create a contradictory being, God also cannot allow for the existence of a perfect being, because a perfect being, in the strict sense of the word, would be God. Hence, no other being, either wholly or in part, can be a totally perfect being. There can be only one pure realization; there cannot be two Gods.

St. Thomas reasons as follows: if the inflexible laws of reality are such that God cannot create a totally perfect being, then the closest possible reflection of perfection that can be realized is the creation of a whole range of beings, from the least perfect to the most perfect. And herein lies a kind of tragedy: the most perfect created being must also be the most fully free, for it will be the most perfect spirit, and, in turn, full freedom consists in the ability of that created spirit to choose good or evil. The possibility of choosing evil is necessary; it cannot be removed from the most perfect spirit. This is the ultimate reason for the trial and rebellion of the angels and also for the trial and rebellion of human beings, both the first humans as well as all the rest of us. Every spiritual creature must undergo the test of freedom.

The essence of evil consists in something lacking a good that it ought to have. Thomas writes: *Privatio est eius quod quis natus est habere et debet habere. In privatione sic accepta est ratio mali (Contra Gent.* III, 6, 1)—privation is a lack of what someone or something by nature, of its essence, ought to have. Privation, thus understood, is the essence of evil. This lack also results from the imperfection of the material factor in the physical world. A great mystery surrounds the dependence of the level of perfection of the material factor on the overall state of the spirit in the world. There are theological theories that say physical evil first began to torment humanity and the world as a result of sins committed by human beings. If original sin did not have the evil effects it does, if humans had behaved differently, then even animals would not be vicious. The well-known friendly attitudes of saints such as St. Francis and St. Jerome toward animals suggest that material values, not to mention the destruction and pollution of the material world, are somehow mysteriously dependent upon spiritual values or the lack thereof.

Evil is always either a lack in the material sphere or a lack of a proper orientation in our knowledge and in the willing connected with this knowledge. The latter is moral evil. Evil—and this is important—is always anchored in something, in some subject, and this subject is good by virtue of the fact that it is a being. Even the greatest evil (recall the problem of Satan, mentioned earlier) always inheres in a subject, which, as a being, is good. Consequently, there is no substantialization or personification of evil. There are no evil things. There are no persons who are evil to the core. There are only material and spiritual privations in good subjects. If we were to search the world over, we would find nothing in existence that is evil. What was said of creatures in the Old Testament at the beginning of the Book of Genesis is still completely true: they are very good. And yet physical and moral evil is something tangible, too! Is God its cause?

God can be regarded as the cause of evil only to the extent that God wills changeable, finite beings. If God did not will such beings, then nothing would exist at all, and it is better to be than not to be, better to exist than not to exist. And so, St. Thomas says: *Deus quasi per accidens causat corruptionem rerum* (*ST* I, 49, 2)—God as though indirectly, *per accidens*, in an accidental way, causes the corruption of things in willing that they exist at all. Things must pass through all the phases of material and spiritual imperfection in order later to arrive at that supernatural state of which faith tells us, the state that will arise *in a new heaven and a new earth*, in a life that is perfect and happy, a life in which everything will be renewed. Tears, suffering, sorrow, and tribulations will all pass away, and only that which is a being, that which is good, will remain. But it is faith that gives us such a vision (see Apoc. 21:1–4); philosophy does not reach that far.

If, however, we are faced with the philosophical problem of the cause of evil, then we should always remember that God, as the cause of all that exists, is the cause of evil *per accidens*. The distinction between *per se* and *per accidens* is important in Scholastic terminology. *Per se* means "of its own essence," and *per accidens* means "indirectly." And so only indirectly, accidentally, and contingently is God the cause of evil. *Per se*, of itself, evil results solely from the imperfection of secondary causes. Secondary causes cannot be perfect because if they did not contain the possibility of many different privations and the consequences thereof they would not be creatures. This is the basic thought that constantly reappears here.

Of course, the preservation of everything in goodness, the abidance of all things, the belief that nothing passes away, that whatever is a being endures, is a vision of faith that also has its justification in philosophy. If something is dependent in its existence on God as the ground of existence, then it is also preserved eternally in this source. What Galczynski once said of Bach, that in Bach you will find everything, can be applied here as well: in God we find everything; all things are in God in an infinitely greater way. Nothing that has come into being, nothing that exists—from the tiniest insect or atom to the greatest spiritual achievements of humans and angels—perishes. Everything abides in God.

This is certainly an optimistic accent, and some might regard it as an oversimplified solution to the problem of evil. But this seems to me to be the only answer because any other solution would necessarily be characterized by Manichaeism. It would require us to accept two sources of being and two kinds of being, the one a source of good and the other a source of evil. Evil would then be substantial—there would be evil things, evil beings; there would be a kingdom of good and a kingdom of evil. Such a view, however, does not stand up to criticism even from a philosophical point of view, and it is fundamentally and radically at odds with faith.

11

The World of Bodies and the World of Spirits

We must consider some rather difficult issues before we take up the question of the human being. Everything around us, all that we see, hear, and touch, everything we can perceive with our senses, makes up the world of material beings. What does St. Thomas think philosophy can tell us about this world? What does philosophy contribute to our understanding of the material world?

Thomas is an adherent of a philosophy that has great confidence in sensory knowledge and holds it in high regard. As we have seen, in Christian thought in general, and in St. Thomas in particular, matter is treated with respect. Christian thought has always been opposed to any disdain for matter. Everything that exists is good. This has always been strongly emphasized by Christian philosophers. The same applies to the senses in relation to knowledge. We will return to this topic in our discussion of the human being.

We humans have both sensory and rational knowledge. If we had no senses, if we were deprived of all the ways by which we normally receive impressions, then we would also not be able to have any rational knowledge in this life. St. Thomas here follows the line of thought clearly marked out by the tradition of Aristotelian philosophy. Sometimes this philosophy is interpreted too biologically, as naturalistic and materialistic. Such an approach is too extreme. Aristotelianism is a type of philosophy that sees the whole foundation of human knowledge in sensory knowledge. This sensory knowledge—sight, smell, touch, hearing, taste—puts us directly in touch only with the world of bodies, the surrounding world of material creatures. No one has ever seen a pure spirit. No one has ever seen God, the most perfect spirit, or any other pure spirit. We can infer the existence of God only on the basis of a certain kind of knowledge concerning our surrounding reality, a knowledge we attain with great difficulty. Sensory knowledge is the point of departure for rational, spiritual knowledge, which is the proper tool that allows us to consider the problem of God and to engage in philosophical, metaphysical contemplation.

Similarly, our faith has its point of departure, its origin, in auditory impressions; it results from what we hear from someone who proclaims the truth of faith. This is clearly stated in St. Paul: *Fides ex auditu* (Rom 10:17). And so here, too, the point of departure is sensory, auditory experience. Through hearing or some other way of receiving the signs that transmit speech to us, we are able to accept the content of that speech. *Fides ex auditu*—faith comes from hearing. These are weighty words. They show what great respect Christian thought has for our humble, dim sensory knowledge, as well as for the whole material world with which we are in constant contact from birth to death and from which we draw our knowledge.

This explains why St. Thomas is so opposed to radical spiritualism, the kind of attitude that, in its view of the world and in its knowledge of reality, belittles or ignores cognitive contact with the material world. A philosopher far removed from Christian thought, Benedict Spinoza, who in the 17th century formulated an extremely logical pantheistic philosophical system that identified God with the world, proclaimed: *I begin my philosophizing from God.* He said contemptuously of the Scholastic philosophers that in their philosophizing they proceeded from things, from tangible, sensory perceptible beings. Descartes, on the other hand, began his philosophical reflection from himself, from his own being, his ego. For St. Thomas, as we have seen, the problem of God lies at the very heart of metaphysics, but—as we shall see when we discuss the Thomistic conception of the human being—all philosophical thought has its roots in sensory knowledge.

The material world, all the material things around us, can be looked at in a variety of ways. A technician, a soldier, a doctor, an artist, a botanist, a chemist, a humanist, and a philosopher will all view this reality in different ways. Here we want to discover what constitutes the uniqueness of the philosophical view of the material world. This will be imperative for us if we are to understand the Thomistic conception of the human being.

Before the time of St. Thomas, the particular sciences strictly speaking did not yet exist. The different disciplines (*artes*) that developed were all included in philosophy. In European thought, the first particular science to break off from philosophy was optics. The famous Polish scholar Witelo, a Neoplatonic philosopher and natural scientist, who may have known St. Thomas personally, played a role in the development of optics. We can take pride in the fact that one of our countrymen was in the vanguard among the thinkers of his day and contributed to the emergence of the first nonphilosophical particular science. The other particular sciences were still blended in a single crucible with philosophy, and it was not until the 15th century that they slowly and gradually separated off from it and began to pursue their own truths and develop independently.

St. Thomas' entire philosophical view of the structure of the material world is based on a thesis already familiar to us and one to which we must constantly return, namely, that all beings are composed of two elements, potential and realization. Let us recall that only God is completely free of all composition. Only in God is there no composition of essence (potential) and existence (realization). God is existence. Everything apart from God is a union of potential, the essence of a given thing, and the realization of this potential, the existence belonging to that thing. Now we must go one step further. The composition of potential and realization, of potency and act, takes place on two levels. All beings, both material and spiritual, with the exception of God, are composed of essence and existence. In spiritual beings such as angels, essence is noncomposite, or simple, whereas in God essence does not differ from existence; it is identical with existence. Angels, therefore, do not have the kind of composite essence that material beings have.

The essence of material beings—and this is a fundamental tenet—is also composed of potential and realization. Consequently, in material beings we find a composition on two levels. The first and more universal is the composition of essence and existence, and the second is a composition within the framework of essence itself. The composition within essence is also a composition of potential and realization, but the potential within the essence of material beings has a distinct nature. It is the potential to be an extended thing, that which we call a body, something that occupies space, is quantitative, quantitatively determinate, measurable, and composed of parts. In the technical philosophical language of St. Thomas' day, this second type of potential was called "matter." We must bear in mind that the term "matter" here means something entirely different from what it means when used by contemporary physicists, natural scientists, and technicians. It is not some sort of already existing raw material but is merely potential, and this potential is something that cannot exist by itself and that is, at the same time, the potentiality to be an extended thing.

The realization of this second type of potential, the potential found in the essence of material beings, is the conferral of the extension of shape in the broadest sense of the term; it is the shaping of this potential primarily in terms of extension. In philosophical language we call this "form." To illustrate this by means of one of the simplest arts, say, the art of pottery, matter would perform the role of the clay to which the potter gives a certain shape, and the role of the shape would here fall to form. But this is not a good illustration because the potential of which we are speaking, unlike the really existing clay, is still not itself a material thing.

According to St. Thomas, then, material beings have a dual composition. They are composed of essence and existence, and their essence is, in turn, composed of matter (the potential to be something extended) and form (the realization of this matter). Matter and form are the constituents that make up the essence of material beings. This is a difficult matter to understand, but we must keep coming back to it, just as we must keep returning to the topic of essence and existence. Unless we reflect upon these matters, we will not be able to understand certain key concepts in St. Thomas' thought, especially those having to do with the human being.

The composition of matter and form—the potential for extension and the realization of this potential—is also referred to as the hylomorphic union, a term derived from Greek. The Greek term *hyle* means matter or raw material, and, literally, it means a forest, the timber from which different objects are produced. That is why the medieval Latinists often translated the word *hyle* as *silva*, forest. *Morphe* in Greek means form or shape. Accordingly, hylomorphism is the view that the essence of all material beings is composed of matter and form. In the course of these discussions, I will frequently use the terms "matter" and "form," but it should always be remembered that they are being used here in the special sense explained above. They are terms taken from the ordinary language of everyday life and, so to speak, endowed and filled with a new philosophical content.

Let us now consider some statements by St. Thomas that specify more precisely how this composition found in all material beings is to be understood.

Everything that surrounds us in the visible world, everything in our sensory perceptible world, is composed of matter and form, understood in the manner explained above. Matter is not some sort of raw material like clay or wood. Matter is something that behaves *like* the clay or wood from which an object is to be made or a container molded; the word "matter" is used here almost metaphorically. St. Thomas emphasizes that just as potential cannot exist without the realization of that potential, without act, so, too, nowhere in the world does matter exist without form. There exist only beings composed of matter and form. *Dicere quod materia est in actu sine forma est dicere contradictoria esse simul, unde a Deo fieri non potest (Quodlibetum* III, 1, 1)—to say that matter is in act without form, to say that matter is realized without realization, is to believe that contradictory things can exist simultaneously, that something can be realized and not realized at the same time, and even God cannot bring this about (*a Deo fieri non potest*). Even God cannot cause matter to exist without form. Matter existing without form, potential realized without realization, is a contradictory object. Matter—and St. Thomas strongly emphasizes this point—cannot exist alone and cannot be created by God because God cannot create contradictory beings.

Forma dat esse materiae, says St. Thomas in *De Principiis Naturae*; form gives existence to matter. Strictly speaking, only God gives existence to the divine creative act that is continually occurring and preserving everything in existence. Matter, however, receives existence from God always through the mediation of form, and that is why St. Thomas says that form gives existence to matter. Matter is a real element of material beings, and, according to St. Thomas, it cannot exist by itself without form. The term "real," we should remember, applies not only to a full-fledged, existing, complete being, but also to the elements that are factors constituting a complete being. Matter is only an element of a being, a factor co-constituting a material being, and not itself a being. Consequently, matter is something real even though it cannot exist alone without form. Matter is not an ideal, imaginary object, an object that is merely a hypothetical, heuristic element. It is, according to St. Thomas, a real component of material beings.

In the material world, only composite beings (*composita, entia composita*), beings composed of matter and form (*composita ex materia et forma*), exist in a subsistent way. The Greek philosophical language had a very expressive name for such beings. They were called *synola*, from *syn*, meaning "together," and *holos*, meaning "whole." A *synolon* is a composite being that is a whole. No material being around us is simply matter or simply form. Each is a composite of these two elements, and each is a certain whole or unity. Of course, God alone, in whom essence and existence are entirely identical, is a perfect unity. All other unities apart from God are increasingly less cohesive, increasingly more tenuous, the closer we come to the material world. Nevertheless, every being has within it a reflection of God's unity. This reflection is sometimes very imperfect because these beings, these mirrors, have different degrees of perfection, and yet they all reflect the perfect unity of God.

St. Thomas, in keeping with a very ancient tradition, enumerates five basic varieties of such unitary, independently existing beings in the material world. There are those who think that this classification is applicable only to the state of physics and the other sciences in medieval times, but it seems to me that this schema is suited to any kind of hypothesis concerning the natural world. After all, these hypotheses are constantly changing and are continually presenting us with new ways of viewing the particular structure of bodies and the material world in general. The five varieties, or classes, of material beings are like the rungs of a ladder, indicating the degrees of perfection among material beings.

On the first rung are the smallest particles, the invisible, imperceptible *synola*. These particles form the most basic canvas, the deepest structure, of all material beings. St. Thomas would never have called them "atoms" because *atomos* means indivisible, and to regard the smallest particles as indivisible is to assume a certain cosmological view; it is to be an atomist in one's philosophy of nature. Thomas is not concerned with stressing that the smallest particles are indivisible. On the contrary, they can be divided to infinity. What is important is that they are the smallest particles. They are the primary *synola*, the lowest material individuals. St. Thomas calls them *corpora elementaria*—the lowest, most basic elements.

The second level consists of the bodies produced from groups of such elementary bodies. We can call them compounds, bodies composed of the smallest bits or particles. They may be referred to by a variety of names taken from the terminology of the particular sciences. The point St. Thomas wants to make is that the second rung of the ladder of material beings consists of compounds produced from the smallest elementary bodies. This is where the inanimate world ends. There are no further inanimate material beings that are subsistent bodies and relatively perfect unities. In Aristotelian terms, such bodies are called substances. A substance is a being that is itself a whole; it exists independently and is the substrate of distinctive properties. In the inanimate world, there are only two kinds of substances. Other beings, such as rocks, clumps of earth, and human products, are not substances in the strict sense of the term. Only beings that are both unitary wholes and independent things, that are truly *synola* and *composita*, are substances, and the only substances in the inanimate world are elements and their compounds.

The third kind of material beings are vegetative organisms. Wherever there is life, from the smallest organism to the most complex, there is already some sort of unity, although this unity is sometimes very tenuous.

The fourth group is made up of animal organisms. It is not the philosopher's task to determine how far the realm of plants extends and where the world of animals begins or where life starts. Those are problems belonging to the special sciences. We will probably never know exactly where these boundaries actually occur. The philosopher only says in a general way where and how they take place. Animal organisms begin where sensory knowledge appears, from the faintest instance of it to the most complex. Many animals surpass us in sensory knowledge. We are well aware that the internal and external senses possessed by certain animals are far superior to our own.

The fifth type of material beings are human beings.

These are the five basic kinds of substances, the five basic types of independent material beings, that St. Thomas, in keeping with a very ancient tradition, enumerates and recognizes as existing in the surrounding world. The distinctions that appeared in this tradition are understood by Thomas in such a way that they ultimately fall into five groups.

In the world in which we live, all material beings can be divided into two realms: natural beings and products. Only the five basic substances —elements, compounds of elements, plants, animals, and humans—make up the realm of natural beings. Everything else in the world is either an animal product or a human product. There is a fundamental difference between the way animals and humans construct their homes, but beavers do build dams, bees build hives, and birds build remarkable nests; these are all products. On the other hand, the unity of even the most ingenious nest or of any other animal or human product is not the unique unity of a substance. A cupboard or a table is not a substance. All of these things belong to the world of products. In the light of philosophical reflection, all human artifacts—buildings, clothes, tools, and all such items of daily use —are aggregates, groups of the smallest elementary substances and of substances that are compounds of elements. Sometimes, along with these inanimate substances, certain plant or animal substances are included in the makeup of products. Often we do not realize that there is a sharp distinction between these two worlds. When we do become aware of it, we look at everything around us differently. There are not many truly natural substances. We are surrounded mainly by products. And these products also have their own type of unity. A table is a certain kind of unity; so, too, is a book, a pencil, and a piece of clothing. The unity that character-izes products, however, is an imposed unity that comes from their producers, the people and animals that make them, and does not result from the very nature of the things themselves. Therein lies the basic difference between these two kinds of beings.

The boundaries between the five basic types of natural material beings mentioned above are very subtle. They cannot be detected experientially; they constantly elude us. The boundary between an animate and an inanimate being is sometimes very difficult to establish; so, too, is the boundary between an element and a compound. Philosophical reflection, however, allows us to see that every minutest being and its manifestations located on a higher level of the five types of natural beings is of infinitely greater worth in terms of perfection than everything found on a lower level. For example, a single manifestation of the most primitive form of life is of infinitely greater value than all the inanimate matter that fills the universe, than all the galaxies combined. Likewise, a single manifestation of knowledge, even the slightest bit of sensory knowledge, is incomparably more perfect than all the biological life not yet endowed with knowledge. So, too, a single act of intellectual knowledge or a single act of free will is of infinitely greater worth than everything on the lower levels. St. Thomas extends this insight to the realm of supernatural life and the order of grace. A single act performed in a state of grace is of infinitely more value than all that occurs in the order of nature.

This hierarchy of beings, this gradational arrangement of values, is sometimes staggering to behold. It helps explain the often amazing perspectives that appear in the different sciences and realms of knowledge. We know, for example, that astronomers are divided into two camps. Some say that there are a great many inhabited planets, that numerous planetary systems such as ours can be found not only in our own galaxy but in other galaxies as well—and there are millions of them. Others ask, Who knows whether the earth may not be unique? Perhaps an immense quantum of inanimate matter was needed to produce somewhere, in the most "remote" corner of the universe, the conditions that would make the appearance of the first signs of life possible. In the light of the hierarchical view presented here, such conjecture ceases to be absurd. The answers to these questions are not given by philosophy. It is for astronomers and other natural scientists to construct hypotheses about life on other planets. But the philosophical problem of the gradations among material beings also gives rise to such questions.

From birth to death we are constantly surrounded by material substances and aggregates or groups of substances—more aggregates, however, than substances because the more human culture develops, the more products there are in our environment and the less contact we have with natural beings. This is quite characteristic of our epoch and of our whole mentality, which is in a certain way marked by this trait. Products are merely aggregates of natural substances. We should recall here that every substance and every aggregate is a unity to a greater or lesser degree. A certain unity organizes each thing into a whole. By nature, an animal is more of a unity and a whole than a plant, and a human being even more so. Aggregates, on the other hand, get their unity from their producers.

A thesis that had far-reaching implications for St. Thomas' conception of the human being was his notion that in every natural substance there is only one form, one realization, that actualizes the substance's potential. In technical language, a being has only one substantial form, one form that constitutes it as a substance. Only one. And so it is wrong to think of the human body as a separate being, like a box or a container, constituted by its own form, and of the soul as another being, which enters the body and lives in it as in a case. This is how we all more or less conceive it. But St. Thomas is radically opposed to such a conception. He regards such a view as naive, magical, and completely contrary to the way things really are. That which constitutes, organizes, and unifies a given substance, that which causes it to be a unity and an independent being, is its substantial form, unique in every substance.

In living beings, and thus also in human beings, we call this substantial form the soul. This statement warrants deep reflection. It presents us with a truth about the human being far from what we normally encounter in religion classes and sermons, and even in our own minds. St. Thomas is very clear on this matter. A single substantial form accounts for everything about a particular being—for the fact that it is a being and that it is a body and, in the case of a plant, that it has life; in the case of an animal, that it has life and sensory knowledge; and, in the case of a human being, that it has life, sensory and rational knowledge, and free will. One substantial form is responsible for all these aspects, from the lowest to the highest, and we call this form the soul. St. Thomas speaks without hesitation of plant and animal souls, as well as human souls. Wherever there is life there is a soul. This soul is not a flame living in the body as in a separately existing container, but is the form that constitutes this container, this bodily organism, and the source of all its functions.

For St. Thomas, then, the soul is not a substance that exists in another substance, a bodily substance. The structure of living beings is not so constituted that it is made up of two substances, one the soul and the other the body. The soul is the principle of life—the principle of a modest life in plants, the principle of a richer life in animals, and, finally, the principle of the richest life in humans, whose souls are able by nature to live on forever. St. Thomas, therefore, defines the soul differently from St. Augustine. Here he follows the Aristotelian tradition rather than the Augustinian. Although he will ultimately agree with St. Augustine, this agreement comes only at the end of the road. At the beginning, he stands in a different place.

For St. Augustine, the soul is primarily a spiritual, rational substance. As a young graduate student, I once participated in a seminar conducted by Professor Gilson. We read various medieval texts on the soul. Whenever the soul was defined as a "rational substance"—*anima est substantia rationalis*—we knew that the author of the text represented the Augustinian tradition. On the other hand, whenever we came upon such phrases as "the rational soul is the form of the body"—*anima rationalis est forma corporis*—it was obvious to us that the text was inspired by the thought of St. Thomas. Thomas also never conceives of the soul as a person. We do not have a person until we have a human being, a whole human being—and that is why death is a rending asunder, and resurrection practically a philosophical necessity. These considerations are extremely important for a proper understanding of St. Thomas' treatise on the human being.

St. Thomas' view that in every substance there is just one substantial form was a new, singular, and "revolutionary" concept in the 13th century. Most of his contemporaries accepted the notion of a multiplicity of substantial forms. It was thought that in the human being, for example, something separately constitutes corporeity, another form establishes sensation, and, finally, a "tiny flame," the substantial rational soul, makes its appearance and, so to speak, crowns those other levels of existence. St. Thomas explicitly rejects such a multiplicity of substantial forms. If he was condemned by certain circles, it was precisely because his teaching on the singleness of form seemed so revolutionary. This teaching was an appeal in behalf of the whole human being, an appeal so incredibly strong in St. Thomas and yet hardly mentioned by Thomists all the way down to the 20th century, when Gilson, Maritain, and others perhaps began to accentuate this aspect of St. Thomas' thought a little more strongly.

St. Thomas, as we have seen, held that the only substantial form in a living being is its principle of life, the soul. The Thomistic view of the world is the direct opposite of the view proposed three centuries later by René Descartes. Descartes said that animals are machines. St. Thomas would reject such a view. He maintained, in contrast, that animals are organisms and not machines, organisms just as marvelous as we ourselves are and even in many cases superior to us. Every organism is a genuine miracle of life and not some soulless piece of machinery. In St. Thomas we find a great respect for the material world in general and for the animal world in particular. Philosophical knowledge of animals is important because we are closely related to them, and this knowledge helps us understand the mechanisms of our own emotional life and sensory cognition. We should know and understand animals in order better to understand ourselves. There is, of course, an essential difference between an animal soul and a human soul. This difference manifests itself primarily in the character of articulated human speech (Thomas' treatment of this matter is perhaps somewhat lacking in clarity). Our ability to speak arises from our ability to form concepts, to judge, and to reason. In animals, St. Thomas admits, we find the beginnings of these functions, but in very rudimentary form. Animals are capable of quasi-reasoning and quasi-judging, but they cannot form concepts. The development of culture is another sign of this difference. Animals do not develop their creative abilities, whereas humans are constantly creating new and extremely diverse things. These are the most striking differences between the activity characteristic of animals and that characteristic of humans.

Medieval Latin thought, in its rich and often marvelous way, pictured the human being as a microcosm, as a small universe in which everything is reflected, the whole wealth of both the material world and the spiritual world. Because we are connected by such strong ties to the whole world, to the material world and to the world of freedom, the world of pure spirits, we are threatened by dangers from both sides, and the effects of these dangers are equally hazardous. We can forget about our ties to the material world or to the world of freedom and spirit. St. Thomas was well aware that Christian thought is constantly threatened from both sides.

Materialism is not a greater danger than radical spiritualism. Both of these extremes must be avoided in order not to lose sight of the truth. We should keep this in mind. Spiritualism asserts that we have within us a spiritual element and emphasizes the priority of this element in the hierarchy of factors that constitute our nature as human beings. Radical spiritualism says, in addition, that our essence consists exclusively in this spiritual factor. While it is true that the spiritual element in us is incomparably more valuable than our sensory and vegetative aspects, nevertheless, to divorce the spiritual from the material is to distort the truth about our nature, and this is very dangerous indeed. The danger of radical spiritualism takes on the familiar form of "angelism," the mistake of confusing human nature with the nature of an angel. We are not mere animals, but we are also not angels; we are human beings. To conceive of ourselves as purely material beings without taking into consideration our higher values, our natural spiritual values, is, therefore, just as great a danger and distortion as to regard ourselves as angels imprisoned in bodies.

St. Thomas, in the teachings that make up his treatise on the human being, constantly reiterates that the union of the soul with the body occurs *ad melius animae*—for the good of the soul. If the soul were an angel, then its union with the body would be to its detriment—*ad peius animae*. Since, however, the human being is a psychosomatic being, the human soul is a principle not of angelic life but of animal life, though of the kind ordained by God for the human being. Consequently, this union is *ad melius*—it occurs for the good. We will return again to these issues when we take up the topic of the human being.

12

Angels (Pure Spirits)

It is worth noting that St. Thomas devoted extensive parts of his writings to matters that are, in fact, as he himself admits, entirely beyond the range of human philosophical experience. Philosophy tells us nothing about angels or about original sin. And yet Thomas devoted a great deal of space to reflections on human beings in the state of innocence (i.e., to the question of how people would look if there had been no original sin) and to treatises on angels. He seems to have written these splendid texts so that we might become better aware of our own state, which is not a state of innocence but a state after original sin, and also so that we might better understand our own nature, which is not an angelic nature but a human nature. In order to arrive at a deeper understanding of human nature, we must have a good understanding of human beings as they were in the divine plan before sin, and we must also have a better understanding of what angels are.

Why did St. Thomas come to be called *Doctor Angelicus*—the Angelic Doctor? Some say it was because of the heroic chastity he exhibited in the face of the difficult ordeals and trials his family put him through to keep him from entering the Dominican Order. Others say it was because of his devotion to the angels, a devotion practiced in the Dominican Order. The Dominicans have a beautiful legend that tells of how angels once came and distributed bread to St. Dominic and his companions when they had nothing to eat. The legend is an expression of the close spiritual ties between the Order of Preachers, particularly in its early days, and the world of angels. Still others suggest that St. Thomas received this title because he was a specialist in angelology, the science of angels. Such speculations notwithstanding, there can be no doubt that St. Thomas concerned himself so zealously with the world of pure spirits because, in the philosophical and theological tradition that held sway in the Latin Christian world, there was often a tendency to confuse human beings with angels. St. Thomas, therefore, was intent upon showing the basic difference that exists between the world of pure spirits and the nature of human beings. This would seem to be the real reason why he devoted his attention to this matter and why he came to be called *Doctor Angelicus*.

Philosophy tells us nothing about angels. We know of their existence only from revelation. Philosophical reflection does, however, incline us to accept their existence as probable. Angels should exist, if we consider the whole hierarchy of the different kinds of beings that populate the universe.

St. Thomas' views concerning angels can be summed up in three points:

1. *The nature of angels.* We have already seen that a pure spirit is not as simple as God. A pure spirit is composed of essence and existence. In the *Summa Theologiae* (I, 50, 2, ad 3), St. Thomas writes: *Licet in Angelo non sit compositio formae et materiae... adhuc remanet comparatio formae ad ipsum esse, ut potentiae ad actum*—although in angels there is no composition of form and matter, because such composition is found only in corporeal beings, yet there is a *comparatio*, a coming together or union of form and existence, and this composition is one of potency and act. In other words, an angel is—to put it in Scholastic language—pure form. There is no matter in an angel. An angel is form, and its essence is to be form alone. Although there is no matter in an angel, no potential to be something extended, there is a composition of essence, which is to be form alone, and existence. This is the kind of composition that occurs in angels.

A multiplicity of individuals (St. Thomas proceeds here like a true Aristotelian) occurs only among material, corporeal beings. Since angels do not have bodies and are not material, there cannot be a multiplicity of angelic individuals. "Angel" is not a species consisting of many millions or billions of individual angels. Theologians are not all in agreement on this point, and this may look like a trivial verbal dispute. But there is something valuable in St. Thomas' view, and it is worth reflecting upon. According to Thomas, every angel is a species that is personified in one exemplar; every angel is an expression of a separate species. It would be the same for us if a single human being expressed the whole of humanity. The differences among angels are, therefore, differences among species, not differences among individuals. This gives us some sense of the inconceivable power, might, and richness of life that resides in the kind of person an angel is.

2. *The knowledge of angels.* Plato thought that human beings were capable of the highest level of knowledge, a type of knowledge he described as the intuition of the essences of things. If we properly train our minds, said Plato, we will be able to perceive the essences of things without the aid of our senses and without the effort of forming concepts,

making judgments, and reasoning. St. Thomas maintained, in contrast, that the ability to know in this way, which Plato attributed to the human mind, is not vested in us during our life in this world. Rather, he said, this is precisely the way of knowing proper to angels. Angels do not need to form concepts or to go through the trouble of reasoning. They know the greatest and most mysterious things simply by gazing at them as at a screen or a mirror in which the essences of these things are revealed. That which we are able to do only through the use of our senses, angels do on the highest level of spiritual knowledge. They know by means of cognitive forms called infused ideas (*notiones infusae*), which are somehow infused into an angel's mind. An angel grasps these ideas effortlessly, whereas we have to work at attaining everything we know.

In his *Commentary on Pseudo-Dionysius'* The Celestial Hierarchy, St. Thomas asks why there are so many choirs of angels, and he answers that it is because there are angels of greater and lesser perfection. Their perfection, in turn, is greater the fewer concepts they need in order to know. Lucifer probably required the least number of concepts. God does not need any concepts. God knows all things in the Word, and the Word is not different from God; the Word is identical with God. We, on the other hand, have to use a whole multitude of concepts. We have a *primitia spiritus*; we are located on the lowest level of spiritual knowledge. An angel knows by means of infused concepts, and all pure spirits have such intuitive knowledge, a knowledge attained without the use of concepts derived from sensory knowledge. We will also have such knowledge after we die, thanks to the light of glory (*lumen gloriae*), but unfortunately we cannot have it here on earth. Whatever is in our intellect must come through the door of our senses. There is nothing in the intellect that has not passed through the senses.

3. *The speech of angels.* In St. Thomas' treatise on angels, we also find a beautiful reflection on the speech of pure spirits, on their movement, and on whom they communicate with. Angelic speech does not have to be articulated like human speech or vociferated like animal speech. Angels communicate by transmitting the content residing within them. *Per simili-tudinem... lingua in eis dici potest vis, qua manifestant aliis quod habent in mente* (*ST* I, 107, 1, ad 2)—we can speak of the language of angels in a metaphorical sense when referring to their power to transmit to others what they have in their minds. Their speech is a transmission or transfusion of concepts from one angel to another.

We ourselves are neither animals nor angels. We are remarkable creatures, unique in our own way. We can change, develop, and improve. Some years after St. Thomas, a great 15th-century philosopher named Pico della Mirandola, who met with an early death, said that human beings are like chameleons because they are constantly changing. But they change only within the scope of their nature. Human nature itself is immutable. Human beings cannot evolve to such a degree that they would turn into either animals or angels. With regard to human nature, we can say what the author of the Letter to the Hebrews said of Christ: *Jesus Christ is the same yesterday, today, and forever* (Heb. 13:8). Similarly, human nature in its essential elements cannot change. As long as the world endures, human beings will remain human beings.

13

What is the Human Being?

Turning now to the topic of the human being in St. Thomas, we will first consider his conception of the human being. Here we will be seeking an answer to the question, What is the human being? Next we will examine human actions, with particular attention to ethics. We will gradually be coming closer to practical concerns. In order for these practical aspects to be really fruitful, however, they must be intelligible, and, in order for them to be intelligible, they must be made accessible through the purely theoretical distinctions presented at the beginning of our study. The theoretical nature of our treatment is still rather illusive since we have not yet introduced the antithesis of theory and practice, especially as it is understood by St. Thomas. These two realms are very intimately related, and fruitfulness in the practical realm depends on the strength of its theoretical foundation. This is also true in the case of the conception of the human being. The metaphysical distinctions that we have already encountered will be indispensable for a good understanding of St. Thomas' thought in the various more practical realms of his philosophy of the human being.

Our treatment of human nature and its aspects will consist of two parts. First we will examine the most important assumptions in St. Thomas' view of the human being, and then we will discuss the eschatological perspectives that result from his conception of human nature. But first a few historical remarks are in order.

In St. Thomas' day, as in our own, there were two extreme views of the human being. One, which was decidedly materialistic in character, was an expression of the 13th-century version of a philosophical theory called somatism. *Soma* in Greek means "body," and somatism is the view that only the body exists. This somatism, which was a form of materialism, said that the human being is nothing but a bodily organism, only more intricate and complex than others that exist in the surrounding world. In ancient philosophy, Democritus, the Epicureans, and the Stoics were the ones who, each in their own way, represented this materialistic view. In the Middle Ages, materialism was not permitted a hearing. Since everything was then sacred, materialism was treated as a heretical view and, therefore, could not be openly proclaimed. Nevertheless, contemporary research has shown that there were closet materialists among the scholars of those days. There were not very many of them, but there were enough to be able to say that the materialistic current in the history of European thought never completely disappeared.

Of course, the prevailing view, which mobilized an enormous number of followers and stood in opposition to materialism, was radical spiritualism, the view that regarded the human being as simply a spirit. The bodily aspect of the human being was seen as accidental and contingent, and a liability. According to this radically spiritualistic view, the human being is a demon, but a demon in the ancient sense of the term, which did not mean an evil spirit. The human being is a spirit that is constrained, confined, and in some way maimed, because it is joined to a body. This radically spiritualistic view, known already toward the close of antiquity, was represented by the followers of Plato in Neoplatonism, a revival of Platonism. Neoplatonism was dominant in the Middle Ages.

Christianized Neoplatonic ideas were always alive and influential, and even today they color our understanding of the human being. Particularly significant in this regard were the views of Origen, Pseudo-Dionysius the Areopagite, and the Arabian philosopher Averroës. According to Origen, a great writer of the early Christian period who was an openly avowed Christian and, at the same time, a Neoplatonist, human beings are angels that sinned by ceasing to contemplate God. As a punishment, these angels were condemned not to hell like Satan for the sin of pride, but only to imprisonment in a body. A sinful angel's sojourn in a body is life as a human being. Human souls are angels condemned to a penitential sojourn in the prison of a body, and they are not set free from this imprisonment until death. After death, humans will again be able to be angels. Thanks to salvation, thanks to penance, they will return to the state of pure contemplation and leave behind all contact with the body. Origin's view is a typical example of angelism. The Greek term for soul, *psyche*, is derived from *psychros*, meaning "cold." The human soul is a cooled down angel that has lost its warmth, its spiritual heat, because it stopped contemplating God.

Pseudo-Dionysius the Areopagite and his great revivalist John Scotus Erigena, who lived in the early Middle Ages during the Carolingian era, represent another view. They approach Neoplatonism as Christians, and they view human nature in more or less the following way: Matter is something evil, and so also is the body. God originally intended for there to be just one human being, Adam. The creation of Eve was already a deviation from the original course, and the multiplicity of human beings even more so. This multiplicity is, according to Erigena, a result of sin. Materiality is also a result of sin. Consequently, the body, sexual differentiation, and the multiplicity of human beings are all evils, and they will disappear in the apocatastasis, in the final return of all things to a perfect individual. There will again be just one human being—Adam. These are the sorts of notions that were promulgated by certain Christian philosophers. John Scotus Erigena was, after all, a famous thinker and scholar during the period that is regarded as the foundation of European culture.

The Arabian philosopher Averroës and his followers also proposed a philosophical view of the human being that attracted adherents. Ibn-Rushd, also known by his Latinized name, Averroës, was one of the greatest Arabian philosophers of the early 12th century. He lived and worked in Cordoba, located in the territory of Spain. Even today, in discussions of the nature and destiny of the human being, we still encounter remnants of his view. We often hear it said, for example, that people die, that people perish, but humanity endures, or that humans are mortal, but the human spirit is immortal. This is precisely what Averroës taught —that there is no individual immortality. Averroës was a true Aristotelian, and in Aristotle the material element is the principle of multiplicity. Only the spiritual element, the human intellect, continues to exist after death, and contact with the material element, the body, is severed. Consequently, the individual intellect, the individual spirit, of each particular human being cannot be immortal and live forever in eternity. After death, all human intellects merge into one angel, forming a single species. This species is what survives, and not individual human beings. Such was the view of Averroës.

All of these views were to a greater or lesser degree alive in St. Thomas' day. He had to respond to the materialistic views that cropped up here and there, as well as to the radical spiritualism that appeared in various forms. The most dangerous and energetic form of the latter was Averroism, which tended to appeal especially to the minds of those in university circles. The interpretation of Averroës' thought presented above was the most popular view in the still young university life of that time. Chesterton, in his monograph on St. Thomas, gives a wonderful description of this situation.[11] Thomas had a difficult task. Faced with these differing—often rather bizarre—views, he sought to retain what in them was true and to develop a view of the human being that seemed to him most accurate.

There was a great temptation then, as there is now, to take the easy way out. The words of Jesus come to mind here: *Not everyone who says "Lord, Lord"* is a true worshipper of God (Matt. 7:21). Similarly, not everyone who is constantly repeating "spirit, spirit" is indicating the most accurate path. We must find the true path, the authentic path, and not the one that only looks as though it is in accord with Christianity. Radical spiritualism—and we owe a great deal to St. Thomas for pointing this out —is a perversion of the authentic Christian view of the human being. It is not a matter of repeating "spirit, spirit" when speaking of the human being, but a matter of presenting the truth about human nature.

What are the main tenets of the view of the human being proposed by St. Thomas in response to the positions mentioned above? Five tenets seem most important and also most characteristic of St. Thomas' view. They include ideas we have already considered.

1. A human being is not a conglomerate of an animal and an angel. A human being is also not a miniature universe or microcosm, in the sense of being a creature in which all the elements of the world occur together. A human being is neither a conglomerate nor a mosaic but a unity. This is a tenet that St. Thomas emphasizes in a most emphatic way, and one that coincides with our contemporary tendency to view the human being holistically (*holos* = whole). The human being is a unity and, moreover, the most perfect being in the visible world of beings composed of matter and a fashioning principle, form. Form and matter, as we have seen, are the elements that constitute a human being. A human being is, therefore, an indivisible whole. It cannot be said, therefore, that the human being is either matter or form (soul, as the principle of life). Consequently, all radical spiritualists who identify the human being with the soul are wrong. Neither the body alone nor the soul alone is a human being. None of the elements, factors, or components that constitute a human being can be said to be the human being. We occasionally find ourselves asking, What in me is actually my self? The self is nothing other than the *synolon*—the whole composed of the elements referred to here as matter and form. The human being is not an aggregate but a unity and a whole.

2. This relatively perfect unity (for only in God is there perfect unity) results from the human being's having just one substantial form, a single fashioning, constituting principle, which is the human soul. The human

being is not a bifurcated creature made up of a soul and a body. As we have already seen, a single substantial form, the rational soul, is the cause of everything in a particular human substance. This form is that which causes the human being to exist, to be a corporeal being, to be alive, to have sensory perceptions, to know in a rational way, and to make free decisions. In other words, the fact that I exist, that I am a being, that I am a living corporeal being capable of receiving sensory impressions, that I know in a rational (and not merely in a sensory) way, i.e., that I can form concepts and judgments and can reason, and that I make free decisions— this is all the work of that one substantial form, that one fashioning principle, called the soul. The soul does not come into an already constituted body as an additional element. Rather, it is the soul that forms the body along with all the body's functions, while also having a spiritual function of its own, one connected with the body but in its essence purely spiritual.

We experience just how strongly these functions are interconnected and how intimately they work together in the concrete acts we perform as living beings when our highest spiritual activities find expression and resonance in our most biological and sensory functions. St. Thomas was perhaps the first to stress so emphatically that the soul endowed with an intellect, the rational soul (which may be called "the intellect" for short), is, in the full sense of the word, the form of the body. In the *Summa Theologiae* (I, 76, 1) we read this very bold assertion: *Necesse est dicere, quod intellectus, qui est intellectualis operationis principium, sit humani corporis forma*—it is necessary to say that the intellect, which is the principle of intellectual activity, is the form of the human body. This was an unacceptable tenet to the Neoplatonists, who radically separated the soul from matter and who regarded the soul as a thing so noble and sublime that it could not be defiled by intimate and lasting contact with the body.

3. It follows, therefore, that the soul's union with the body cannot be an accidental union, as Origen would have it. St. Thomas rarely becomes exasperated with anyone, but he loses his patience with Origen. Till the end of time, says St. Thomas, we will feel the fatal consequences of so erroneous a teaching as Origen's doctrine of the human being . The soul's union with the body, says St. Thomas, cannot be a contingent, accidental union. It must be an essential, substantial union, a union that genuinely constitutes the human substance as a unity. We ought not say that the soul

resides in the body, that it lives in the body—these are inaccurate expressions. The soul produces its home; it weaves its body. The union of the soul with the body, which is the union of a substantial form with matter, is precisely what constitutes, what produces, a concrete human being. The human soul is not by nature an angel, although it has, like an angel, the highest spiritual cognitive and appetitive functions. The soul is not an angel for whom it is proper by nature to exist without a body. St. Thomas, as we have seen, emphasizes that the union of the rational soul with the body is the realization of human nature and is for the soul *ad melius*—for its good, and not *ad peius*—to its detriment. He is responding here to views that disparaged the value of the body. Of course, if the soul were an angel and were united only contingently to the body, this union would then be *ad peius* for the soul, to its detriment; it would be a degradation for the soul.

When speaking in this context of the human soul, St. Thomas frequently uses the term *humanus intellectus*—the human intellect. Sometimes this term refers exclusively to the cognitive power, but often it includes the appetitive power as well. In the human being there are always both cognitive and appetitive functions (the word "appetitive" need not be understood here in the ethical sense; appetitive functions are simply desires). And it is just this astonishing substantial form, this *humanus intellectus*, united in the human being in a natural way with the body, that *est infimus in ordine intellectuum et maxime remotus a perfectione divini intellectus (ST* I, 79, 2)—that is the lowest in the order of intellects in the spiritual world and the remotest from the perfection of the divine intellect. There is a gradation here: the divine intellect, which is identical with the divine essence, is the highest intellect, and then, as we have already seen, there are various levels of angels, who are more or less perfect depending on whether they employ a greater or lesser number of cognitive forms in order to know.

This was how St. Thomas interpreted the matter, based on Pseudo-Dionysius' view of the celestial hierarchy. *Anima... nostra in genere intellectualium tenet ultimum locum sicut materia prima in genere sensibilium (De Veritate* X, 8)—in the order of spiritual beings, says St. Thomas, the human soul occupies the lowest place, like prime matter in the order of corporeal beings. He, therefore, sees in human beings, in human nature, the first glimmerings of rational, spiritual life. In humans these glimmerings are the lowest, and in angels they are incomparably

more perfect, to say nothing of God, who is infinitely superior to everything. The human soul is located *in confinio spiritualium et corporalium
creaturarum* (see *ST* I, 77, 2)—on the boundary of spiritual and material
creatures. The soul is what brings these *primitiae spiritus*—these first
glimmerings of spiritual life—to the human being.

4. A human being is both an individual and a person. This issue has
been the subject of extensive investigations by such scholars as, for
example, Jacques Maritain, one of the greatest contemporary exponents of
St. Thomas' thought, and has implications for our life in society. A human
being is constituted of matter and form. Each of us is an individual thanks
to the material factor in us. There are millions of human beings now alive,
millions who have gone before us, and millions more who will come after
us. All of these millions of individuals are human beings and belong to a
single species, the human species. Each of us is a person thanks to the
spiritual factor in us, the rational soul, which is endowed with rational
life—spiritual knowledge and desire. This is precisely what makes us
persons. Although the soul is the principle of personality, it is not itself a
person. Only the complete human being is a person.

These are not trivial matters from the point of view of eschatology. As
philosophers, who do not have recourse to revelation, we can have a
rationally grounded conviction that the human soul, the factor that
constitutes the human being, is immortal. If, however, the human being is
to be immortal, then the whole person must be immortal, and the immortality of the soul is still not the immortality of the person. There is,
therefore, a kind of philosophical necessity for the resurrection. The resurrection is not a philosophical truth because philosophy can say nothing
about it, and yet, on the basis of the conception of the human being
developed by St. Thomas, the resurrection is in a sense suggested. If the
human being is immortal, then the immortality at issue must be the
immortality of the whole human being, the immortality of the human person. The issue of the immortality of the human soul and of the consequent
immortality of the whole human being will become clearer when we take a
closer look at rational cognitive human activity. St. Thomas discusses
these matters in great detail. For him the immortality of the soul is not just
a truth of faith but a *revelabile*, a truth that is also accessible to us philosophically. We should note here, however, that there were important
Christian theologians who were of a different opinion. For example, Duns
Scotus, the great Franciscan theologian and philosopher, maintained that

the immortality of the human soul is solely and exclusively a truth of faith. It can be accepted on the basis of faith but not as a result of philosophical reflection. St. Thomas takes a different position.

5. The presence in us of purely spiritual powers and activities is what allows us to assert the immortality of our principle of personality and consciousness, the principle constituting us—our soul. Our substantial form does not perish, and neither does that which St. Thomas calls the commensurability of each soul to a particular body. I wrote my habilitation thesis on St. Thomas' doctrine of the *commensuratio animae ad hoc corpus*—the commensurability, or conformity, of each soul to this body.[12] I will not here go into the extremely complicated and difficult consideration of such questions as, What is meant by "this body"? What is meant by "commensurability to this body"? In general, however, we may understand this to mean that a particular soul—yours, mine, and everyone else's—can and must, taking matter from anywhere in the world (for prime matter is everywhere), constitute only this particular body and no other. We are constituted in such a way that it belongs to the nature of our substantial form, our soul, to be united with a body. Moreover, each soul is precisely commensurate to a particular body. In other words, a soul cannot constitute any other person than the one it has already once constituted. This is a fundamental tenet. This does not mean that in the next world we have to be identically and physically just as we are here and now. We must, however, be exactly these same persons.

Viewed in this light, any kind of metempsychosis or transmigration of souls makes absolutely no sense. If there were several consecutive deaths, and if after each one the human soul were joined to a new body, then, according to St. Thomas, the same human being would have to be reconstituted each time. A soul cannot pass from one body to another as from one room to another or one house to another. Within the essence of each soul resides the constituting of this body and no other. The notion of the transmigration of souls is conceivable only within some radically spiritualistic view, such as Neoplatonism.

St. Thomas' doctrine of *commensuratio* is very important. It points to the commensurability of each human soul to a particular fetus, to this particular, tiny, developing human being, who contains his or her full range of genetic endowments and in whom resides *in nuce*, embryonically, the whole future human being. The soul created by God is suited to this fetus in the mother's womb. This commensurability is eternal and cannot be expunged from the human soul. St. Thomas is very emphatic about this. If the soul continues to exist, then so must the whole human being, and no other but this particular concrete human being. Many questions arise here. What do we mean by "this human being"? After all, each of us is constantly changing from the moment we are an embryo in our mother's womb until the moment we die. What does this commensurability mean concretely? We know that we are constantly changing, but we also realize that there is something in us that endures, and this "something" is the soul with its commensurability to this body.

14

The Eschatological Destiny of the Human Being

For many philosophers—especially those who philosophize in the spirit of Plato—philosophy is a meditation on death, a *meditatio mortis*. This is one of the many names given to philosophy. Death is such a significant event for human beings that the understanding of it, to the degree that this is possible, has always been regarded as extremely important. In materialism, death is the end of all consciousness and existence. In spiritualism, death is the release of the soul from its imprisonment, a vacating of its bodily shell, a sundering of its connection with the body.

From a purely natural point of view, death is a cataclysmic event. It is a rending apart of the unity that each of us is. Faith tells us that this kind of death comes to us as a result of original sin. Materialism is correct to the extent that the whole human being, like other corporeal substances, is destructible. The seamless union of matter and form disintegrates.

But philosophical reflection tells us that there abides in us a strange, divine, indestructible element. In European philosophy, several hundred years before Christ, Plato and Aristotle had already drawn attention to the presence in the human being of something divine (*theios*), something that transcends the body. Thanks to this factor, the soul, the form constituting the human being, can continue to exist after the destruction of the psycho-somatic human individual, although after this sundering, this separation from the body, the soul can perform only part of its functions. It can only perform intellectual and volitional acts. It cannot, however, perform sensory and biological functions, because these can be realized only when there is a complete *compositum*—a body-soul composite existing as a substance.

The soul in its existence after death is not a complete human being or a complete person. And so it yearns, so to speak, for reunion with the body and for complete humanness. The soul has knowledge and life but has them as though it were an angel of the lowest rank. If the soul existing after death is not a complete human being and not a complete human person, then the corpse is not a body. The corpse is a relic, an aggregate of cells that constituted a substantial unity when the soul enlivened them. St. Thomas says that the only reason we call a corpse a body is because it outwardly resembles a body, but it is no longer the body of a human being. In contrast, we can say that Jesus' body was really in the tomb, because he was a complete personality even after he died, since there is always in him the same one Person, the Divine Word. If Jesus were only a human being, we could not say that his body was in the tomb.

In the purely natural order, the rational soul's existence after death is an expectation of wholeness, an anticipation of the realization anew of the complete human being. This natural expectation of a renewed realization of the complete human person may be described as a yearning for resurrection, for complete existence, and, ultimately, for God, a yearning that is even stronger in the natural order after death than during life. We need not, however, stop at this natural perspective, for it is infinitely transcended by the supernatural vocation of the human being.

The human soul survives death. This truth is for St. Thomas, as we shall see, even a philosophical certainty. And yet the separation from the body brought about by death is still a very significant event, since by it the human being ceases to be a complete person. The soul awaits and necessarily requires a complete personality, and so it also awaits and requires the resurrection.

We may also view this whole issue from another perspective, from that of the question of the endurance of reality as a whole. Only God is absolutely eternal and indestructible. All creatures, in contrast, are relatively indestructible; they do not have the kind of absolute indestructibility that belongs to God alone. Because, however, they have come into being and are rooted in God, in the very reason of existence, in self-subsistence existence itself, they endure in God as their cause. Whatever is a being endures in God as the source of its existence. Conscious beings—angels and humans—endure in God differently than beings devoid of consciousness, but everything that exists endures in God in some way. For human beings, beings in whom a spiritual element resides, death is a release from this spatiotemporal order, a transition to a different time and a different space. This is extremely difficult and, strictly speaking, impossible to imagine, and yet in another sense it is obvious that, in leaving the spatiotemporal continuum in which we now live, we will cross over into another order. These matters take on a different meaning when considered in the light of revelation.

In the natural order, a human soul existing after death without a body is in an impaired and incomplete state, a state of waiting, so to speak, and yet it is also in a kind of spiritually purified state. Those who are redeemed at the moment of death become real participants in the divine life; they begin to participate in the life of God. They do not enter some other interim order of time and space but enter eternity, which is beyond time, and participate in the life of God, the life of the Trinity. Eternity, as I said, is beyond time. A logical consequence of St. Thomas' doctrine (though he himself does not directly state it) seems to be that the redeemed do not have to await the resurrection, because in God there is an eternal "now." The condition, and even the necessity, of awaiting the last judgment and resurrection is peculiar to creatures existing in space and time. In the divine order, however, everything already is. When we enter into a real participation in God, we will be able to say of ourselves what St. Paul foretold: *I shall know even as I am known* (1 Cor. 13:12). Those who have been redeemed already exist as persons and are already participating in everything that for us who live in this temporal, spatial, earthly order may take place over the course of millions or billions of years. This is a perspective that helps us view the imperfection of the existence of the soul separated from the body in a new and more positive light, because it shows us that this imperfection applies only to those who have not yet been redeemed.

I shall not discuss the purely theological topic of purgatory. It is clear from revelation, however, that those who are not in purgatory, but are already redeemed, pass beyond the state of unhappy longing and incomplete personality. Their souls are no longer separated from their bodies but are already in a state of resurrection, and this "already" means that they are beyond time. The redeemed who participate in the life of God also regain everything that is a being, because everything that exists—everything that is good and true and beautiful—endures. In the familiar words of the Apocalypse, *there will be no mourning or weeping or pain* (Apoc. 21:4), because all such things are an expression of the state of imperfection. Everything will be new, and the old order will pass away. Jesus said of the wine at the Last Supper: *I shall drink new wine in the kingdom of heaven* (see Luke 22:18). I take these passages to be speaking of a state in which absolutely everything will be recovered, including our existence as fully resurrected and complete persons.

This, I believe, provides an important corrective to the way in which this matter is usually understood. St. Thomas' treatment of the soul's existence after death leaves something to be desired. The picture we are left with is not very appealing: that of a poor soul, wandering around without a body, and living a life worse than our own, while we have a complete life! Such a soul, it is true, has purer cognitive and volitional functions than ours, but it is not a full personality. In the case of the souls of those who are not yet redeemed, St. Thomas' description seems fully warranted. Those who are redeemed, however, participate in the life of God. They do not await the last judgment (as we do in this world), but already share in the resurrection. We know from revelation that this participation in divine life is real. Those who are redeemed are already living with us and with all who will be redeemed from now until the end of time, because for God everything is a present moment; there is no before or after. *Aeternitas*—eternity—is not a time that lasts forever but simply a "beyond-time." This beyond-time belongs neither to us nor to pure spirits —only to God. And yet St. Paul tells us that *eye has not seen and ear has not heard what God has prepared for those who love God* (1 Cor. 2:9), and he also says, *I shall know even as I am known* (1 Cor. 13:12). This means that I shall know just as I am known by God. I shall participate in divine knowledge and in divine life.

Revelation opens before us dizzying perspectives. We need not worry that certain important or beautiful experiences will pass away, because everything *is*, everything endures. Only all that is nonbeing—and now we are returning to philosophy, which is helpful here—will disappear. Evil, ugliness—these are nonbeing. Viewed in this light, the words of the Apocalypse are incredibly profound. *There will be no mourning or weeping*, because these are nonbeing and do not endure. On the other hand, the whole of creation will in some way participate in this new life. As the Fourth Eucharistic Prayer proclaims: *Then in your kingdom, freed from the corruption of sin and death, we shall sing your glory with every creature*. Everything that is not evil, corrupt, or depraved will be with us because, as a being, it exists in God.

These things are very difficult to understand. We do not find them addressed directly by St. Thomas, but the kinds of conclusions I have presented above can be derived from his philosophy as a whole.

One final point deserves mention here. Thomas is opposed to Neoplatonism and to other radically spiritualistic views for yet another reason. Even among non-Christian Neoplatonists, certain kinds of mysticism and spirituality are practiced. Although this is a natural mysticism, its principles proclaim that we can, with great inner effort and asceticism, achieve a kind of spiritual life that is in some way a transition to the other world. We also encounter this notion among the great Hindu mystics.

St. Thomas is decidedly opposed to such a view. He says that there is an impassable chasm between what we are capable of here in our present condition—even in our loftiest spiritual achievements and mystical experiences—and what awaits us in the next life. This is also why he maintains that we will need a special spiritual power in order to see God and to participate in God's *aeternitas*. He calls this power the *lumen gloriae*, the light of glory. Without it we would not be able to experience what St. Paul promises awaits us. Between our reality, our present possibilities, and what will belong to us when we enjoy eternal happiness, there is not merely a difference of degree but a difference of kind, an essential difference. A completely new order awaits us, one that infinitely surpasses all that we are capable of here, even with the greatest effort on our part. We will need that *lumen gloriae*, that light of glory, to be able really and consciously to participate in divine life. The doctrine of the *lumen gloriae* is very specifically Thomistic.

15

Basic Features of St. Thomas' View of the Human Being

To fully understand St. Thomas' view of the human being, we must appeal constantly to certain fundamental concepts in his philosophy of being. Without them, without a firm grasp of them and constant recourse to them, his doctrine of the human being will be for us just a set of formulas, and we will fail to appreciate its full meaning. Among the basic concepts we must constantly keep in mind are potential and realization, essence and existence, and matter and form.

As we have seen, the concepts of matter and form—the material element and the element that fashions that material—play an especially important role in understanding the human being. For St. Thomas, the human being is not a soul, but a whole composed of a material element and a fashioning element, which is the soul. In each of us there is a single soul, and it is this soul, this fashioning element, that makes us a human being. This element, this single form, accounts for the presence in us not only of our intellect and free will, but of all of our powers, from our lowest biological functions to our highest spiritual abilities. In technical language, we call this form the substantial form; it is the form that fashions, constitutes, and determines a human being as a whole.

Let us first consider two basic features of St. Thomas' philosophical anthropology (*anthropos* in Greek means "human being"). After this general overview, we will turn our attention to the activity characteristic of every human being.

We know that for St. Thomas everything that exists is good. Everything that exists, exists only because it is an object of divine love; it would not exist if God did not love it. This is a primary principle of St. Thomas' entire philosophy and theology: everything that exists is good. Evils are merely lacks that result either from the natural physical imperfection of beings or from moral evil. Consequently, only physical and moral lacks are evil, and nothing that surrounds us is evil of its own nature.

The whole world is good: the whole world of creatures and the whole world of culture, all that we create and all that we contribute to the existing world through our various modes of human activity. This principle is extremely important. Perhaps St. Francis did not realize how much of a philosopher he was when he sang his hymn in praise of creation. This affirmation of goodness is the source of the deepest optimism: there is no place for evil as a being, and, in the eschatological perspective, everything must be good, beautiful, and wonderful because evil will ultimately disappear completely.

We need to be aware of this, because it has important ramifications for our spiritual life, our asceticism, our spirituality. Regardless of whether we belong to the religious or to the lay state, our spirituality ought to reflect a positive attitude toward the whole of reality, toward the world as a whole. For this reason, too, all disdain for matter, for the body, for certain seemingly insignificant things—is fundamentally unchristian. Nothing may be an object of our contempt, everything must be an object of our love, because it is an object of divine love, it is a being, it is good. Everything is loved by God. Lack and perishability are evil; in the final analysis, however, only sin is truly evil. Given this view of reality, St. Thomas stands out as an adversary of two tendencies, each of which, in its own way, is contrary to this radically positive attitude, namely, Manichaeism and sacralism.

Manichaeism was a religion that occupied vast regions of the Asiatic, African, and European continents. It became a rival of Christianity during the early Christian era, especially in the days of St. Augustine. It was strongly influenced by Persian religious beliefs, and it treated the question of good and evil very differently from Christian thought. Manichaeism takes its name from Mani, its founder, who taught that two powers govern the world, or else one God with a dual nature. These two powers were the principle of positive good and the principle of positive evil. Manichaeism attained great popularity in the days of St. Augustine, who was for many years himself a follower of the Manichaean faith before converting to Christianity. Manichaeism became a catalyst for debates about good and evil and for promoting the view that evil exists in a positive sense.

In Manichaeism, many aspects of which found their way into the culture of the Mediterranean basin, we find the source of the frequently heard negative appraisals of such things as marriage, sexuality, the body, material goods, and, in general, the whole earthly realm. The Manichaean outlook on life gave rise to an attitude of disdain and aversion for such things, which it regarded as belonging to the kingdom of Satan. Christianity does not deny that Satan has influence in the world, but evil should never be treated as a positive factor, and still less as a power governing the world parallel to the power of good. Thomas was a fervent foe of such a dualistic conception of good and evil. During his lifetime and throughout the medieval era, as in the early years of Christianity, Manichaean views continued to survive and spread.

Time and again over the course of history we find attempts to condemn marriage and sexuality and everything connected with them based on the assumption that people ought to lead a life of total abstinence, that marriage is essentially evil, and that this whole realm is contemptible and may, at best, be merely tolerated. The church has always defended a different position, and yet every now and then this tendency reappears. This entire discussion was revived during the Middle Ages in connection with certain heresies that arose in the centuries immediately preceding St. Thomas, namely, the heresies of the Cathari, the Albigenses, and others, who, unfortunately, were so severely persecuted "with fire and sword" that the wounds then inflicted upon them are to this day still bleeding in France. In St. Thomas' time, the spirituality of the Cathari, whose name means "the pure," still persisted and held its ground, while Manichaeism maintained a strong base in the Balkan Peninsula, and from there infiltrated other European countries.

St. Thomas took a clear and unequivocal stance in relation to such views: there is no dualism of good and evil. Everything that exists is good. The whole human being is good—not just the soul, but the entire person. At the same time, only God is completely good; only God is a pure good. All created beings, all creatures without exception, are encumbered with certain lacks. Consequently, evil is found throughout the world. We are reminded here of Jesus' words: *Why do you call me good? No one is good except God alone* (Luke 18:19). These words reveal the truth that there are lacks everywhere. Revelation also, however, sheds clear light on the fact that there are only two human persons without sin: Jesus and the immaculately conceived Mother of God. Even the greatest saints are burdened with sin. The church is a society of sinners. An awareness of the universality of good and, at the same time, of its imperfection and mixture with evil is extremely important. It opens up stimulating perspectives on humanity as a whole, on the People of God, who are the church, and on each human being. Despite the lacks and deficiencies, everything that surrounds us is fundamentally good. This truth gives rise to the necessity of treating every creature with profound respect, a respect we find clearly in evidence throughout the works of St. Thomas.

Here at Laski, a life-giving synthesis of the spirit of three saints—Thomas, Francis, and Benedict—is supposed to prevail. In his respect for the whole of creation and for every creature, St. Thomas reveals a similarity—one frequently overlooked—to St. Francis, who was distinguished by his exceptional respect for every most insignificant animal and plant. Every speck of dust, everything that exists, ought to be an object of our respect, because in it is always some good, in it is the splendor of God. The Franciscan spirit is certainly not opposed to the Dominican spirit that St. Thomas represents; these spiritualities mutually complement one another. Francis expresses in a different, more poetic, human, and affective way the same truth that lies at the basis of Thomas' doctrine. In both we are struck by their attitude of reverence for every creature without exception.

Because this respect embraces the whole human world, the whole *regnum hominis*, it also embraces the whole world of human culture—all the things we create and all the things with which we supplement the world of nature. Here the spirit of St. Francis and St. Thomas converges with the spirit of St. Benedict. The Benedictines see an "everlasting stroke of the chisel" in every most insignificant activity. Whether we happen to be sweeping a floor, illuminating a manuscript, participating in the liturgy, creating a scholarly work, or doing chores in a barn—all these things, from the perspective of Benedictine spirituality, have everlasting value. This corresponds to the earlier mentioned eschatological view that whatever is positive, whatever is a being, endures. If God does not forget a single hair that falls from a person's head, still less will God forget any of the most insignificant tasks we perform. There are no jobs and no things deserving of contempt. This awareness gives rise to a solicitude for small and supposedly transitory things, a solicitude that I always so admired in Father Kornilowicz. He had a great reverence for everything, for things that, in the perspective of some spiritualities, might seem of little importance. They are, however, all important, because they all go to make up one great edifice, whether it be the world of nature or the world of culture.

This is why it is so important to be able to see good in every human being. When someone once remarked to Father Chenu, who was a great authority on St. Thomas, that the last Vatican Council had deviated far from St. Thomas' thought, Chenu replied that this Council, although it said little about St. Thomas, was one of the most Thomistic councils in all of history. I believe this is an accurate observation. John XXIII, who to a large extent inspired the spirit that prevailed at the Second Vatican Council, said that one of the principles by which he tried to live was the thought that, whenever we engage in a dialogue with someone, regardless of who that person is, we should always remember that this person is definitely superior to us in some respect, even if we happen to be dealing with the most notorious sinner or with someone judged or reputed to be perverted or depraved. And he is right.

This anti-Manichaean stance, which finds expression in a positive, realistic, affirming attitude of reverence not just for every human being but for every creature and every thing, is the first basic feature of St. Thomas' thought to which I wish to draw attention here.

The second feature, St. Thomas' opposition to sacralism, is more difficult to understand. "Sacralism" is an ambiguous word. It is derived from the Latin term *sacrum*, which means "sacred," "holy," "consecrated," "set apart for religious purposes." In the wake of Vatican II, this word began again to be more widely used, and it can help us understand a certain attitude very characteristic of St. Thomas. Sacralism may be understood as either a positive or a negative phenomenon. In discussions of recent years, this term has generally been used in a pejorative sense. It then refers to the view that there exists a separate sphere of issues and objects connected with worship, prayer, and spiritual life, a so-called "sacred" sphere, that deserves particular interest and respect on the part of believers. Everything else, all that belongs to the so-called "nonsacred" side of reality, to the secular sphere of life, and is not stamped, so to speak, with this mark of the sacred, is at most to be tolerated, but is basically unimportant in relation to the sacred and not deserving of attention and concern. On the surface, this view may seem beautiful and proper, since it extols the sacred side of existence. In reality—and this is very important—such sacralism is a deformation of Christianity, not unlike Manichaeism. It is an expression of "ghetto" Christianity and, in a bad sense, of sacristy and cloister Christianity, the mentality that looks upon the entire temporal world as a necessary evil, as a certain *malum necessarium*.

Such an attitude gives rise to the tendency to divorce the sphere of worship, prayer, and contemplation from the whole sphere of temporal concerns, and to view the former as alone worthy of reverence and respect and the latter as something that of necessity must be tolerated, but that is basically deserving of contempt. This is a danger that threatens all Christians, and perhaps especially those in religious life. Sacralism in this sense, where all our spiritual attention is concentrated on the sphere of worship and prayer, combined with a disdain for and devaluation of other matters, is foreign to the spirit of St. Thomas, for whom everything, every matter in its own order, is sacred. There is no division into the sacred and the nonsacred. Everything is sacred—and this is the tenet of authentic sacralism. Let us recall the words of St. Paul: *Whether you eat, or drink, or whatever else you do, do it all for the glory of God* (1 Cor. 10:31).

And so everything is sacred. Everything should be saturated with the spirit of God, both the most sublime contemplative prayer and the most humble domestic task. Strictly speaking, therefore, we should not introduce a sharp boundary between contemplation and praxis. These two spheres should intimately permeate one another. Someone once wrote an article on the topic of theory and praxis in St. Thomas, showing that the sharp opposition that appears between these spheres in Aristotelianism is presented in an entirely different way in St. Thomas.[13] This, then, is how St. Thomas' attitude toward human affairs should be understood; such was the attitude of Father Kornilowicz, and such was also the spirit that pervaded Vatican II. The continuity of this whole line of thought is striking. Everything has eternal worth, even though the form of this world shall pass away.

Maritain once said that St. Thomas is a prophetic saint, one who casts light upon a future age. St. Thomas' thought, however, has not yet born its proper fruit. It has born fruit, but unfortunately often in an improper sense, a triumphalistic, ideological sense, rather than in the way it should. The value of St. Thomas' anthropology has still not been fully appreciated. He is also not a product of medieval feudalism. He is a figure who transcends his age and opens up perspectives for the future. Perhaps—as Maritain, Gilson, and, no doubt, also Cardinal Journet believed—ours is the epoch in which his thought is to bear fruit. The founders of Laski understood this well, acknowledging Maritain's great contribution in pointing out that in St. Thomas we find a drive toward autonomy and a full appreciation of the temporal.

The whole sphere of temporal life—every occupation, every kind of work, the entire realm of marriage and family life, physical labor, scientific and aesthetic pursuits, the beauties of an ordinary day, and all the other rich and diverse aspects of secular life—should be appreciated because it all has value and it all serves to build up the church. Everything becomes sacred when it is permeated with the spirit of the Gospel; everything—and not just the sphere consecrated to matters of worship or connected with the inner life. The separation of these spheres is one of the symptoms of Manichaean dualism. To understand properly St. Thomas' approach to spirituality, we must constantly bear in mind these two points: his anti-Manichaeism and his understanding of sacralism. In Thomistic spirituality, we find a different outlook on the world from that which gained acceptance in the modern age and a different understanding of what it means to view reality from a Christian perspective.

We have something to learn from St. Thomas, St. Francis, and St. Benedict, these truly great figures who, in key areas, established for us foundations still intact in their strength. They left us with a vision in which the whole human realm, the *regnum hominis*—the whole human being and all human endeavors—attains its full value. This realm is distorted and loses its value only when the order is disturbed, which occurs when human ends become ultimate ends. We then fall victim to what Maritain called anthropocentric humanism, the view that regards the human being as the center of everything (*anthropos* means "human being," and *centrum* means "center"). We advance toward our fullness in theocentric humanism, the kind of humanism that regards God as the ultimate end. Whether we live in a religious congregation or in a family household, whether we spend our time doing philosophy or theology, caring for the blind, or housecleaning, makes no difference at all. Our main task is to introduce everywhere the ideal of theocentric humanism. This theocentric humanism, so different from sacralism in the pejorative sense, is the ideal toward which St. Thomas' whole teaching on the human being leads. This teaching may also serve as a general introduction to Thomistic spirituality. St. Thomas' works present us with not only an anthropology but also a corresponding spirituality, one very characteristic of this great Doctor.

16

Human Activity

We have already discussed the nature of the human being, and so we know that the human being is a substance, a being that is a unitary whole composed of prime matter, a material principle, which is the bodily aspect, and substantial form, a fashioning principle, which is the soul. Now we shall turn our attention to human activity.

St. Thomas' philosophical and theological thought is decidedly theocentric, concentrated on the question of God, but it is also very humanistic as well. In order to know and love God as fully as we are able, we must strive to understand the human being as well as we can. The two are interrelated and interdependent. Likewise, the better we understand the human being, the easier it will be for us to understand the mechanism of human activity. The philosophical concept of human nature and its aspects will be indispensable to us here, because the word "nature" signifies the constant and unchanging foundation of a being's activities. Every human being, each of us, has a human nature. This nature is what accounts for the fact that we are human beings, and not some other kind of animal, and for the fact that our activities take place in us as they do, and not in some other way.

We cannot derive this theory, this general understanding of human activity, from contemporary psychology or sociology, because these disciplines have become nonphilosophical sciences, and, as such, they investigate phenomena rather than the ultimate reasons for these phenomena. They leave to philosophy an explanation of why human beings behave as they do, in terms of the ultimate reasons residing in human nature that account for the various modes of human activity. Contemporary psychology no longer deals with the concept of nature or with the various intellectual, cognitive, appetitive, sensory, rational, etc. powers. This is neither good nor bad. Psychology has simply become a different type of science, and, like other such sciences, it needs to be supplemented by philosophy. We cannot, therefore, expect contemporary sociology or psychology, as particular sciences, to tell us what we want to know about the human being from the philosophical side. The only way we will arrive at such knowledge is by applying the philosophy of being, i.e., metaphysics, to the question of the human being.

St. Thomas, in his conception of human activity, follows the ancient Greek philosophical tradition formulated by Aristotle. According to this tradition, there are three spheres of human activity: knowledge, conduct, and creativity. The Greek names for these three basic kinds of activity are *theoria*, *praxis*, and *poiesis*. *Theoria*, the first type of activity, goes far beyond the realm of science. Originally *theoria* did not mean "theory" in the sense of a scientific structure, but contemplation. *Theorein* means to look at, to gaze upon, and so *theoria* refers to a contemplative attitude. *Praxis*, the second type of activity, refers to an active attitude, which finds expression in human conduct. This is the realm that forms the subject matter of ethics. *Poiesis*, the third type of activity, is pure creativity. The meaning of the word *poiesis* here is not restricted to poetry in the sense of written verse, but encompasses any and all creative activity. This creativity brings about the world of culture—the totality of human products, both material and spiritual. To this realm belongs all artistic and technological creativity.

In ancient times, the human being was called a miniature universe, a microcosm (*mikros* in Greek means "small," and *kosmos* means "universe"). Most thinkers, including St. Thomas, interpreted this to mean that the human being is a microcosm because within this being three kingdoms converge: the kingdom of plants, the kingdom of animals, and the kingdom of pure spirits, or angels. In the Middle Ages it was said that *homo est in horisonte*—the human being is at the horizon, at the intersection ("horizon" at that time meant intersection or boundary). The human being is a kind of boundary zone where three worlds intersect. St. Thomas makes frequent reference to our intimate kinship with these three kingdoms. Here again we find a remarkable convergence between the views of St. Thomas and St. Francis. Our kinship with all living things and with the whole of nature seems particularly in need of emphasis today, in view of the horrible barbarity we often see exhibited in this sphere. We lack that friendly relationship to the world that characterized St. Francis and that attitude of respect for every existing thing that distinguished St. Thomas.

Thomas, following Aristotle, says that the most basic functions of our organism unite us with the world of plants. All of these functions are the work of one and the same immortal, spiritual substantial form—the soul.

This soul, in conjunction with the material factor in us, performs the lowest biological functions in our organism. Thomas appeals to the metaphysical theory of potential and realization to explain how these functions occur. The activities of a living being take place through the realization of the potentialities residing in it. These potentialities are various powers: intellectual powers, powers of behavior, powers of creativity, etc. They also include specifically biological powers. When activities that are in potency pass from potency to act—to use the technical language—they are realized.

We find biological powers in all living beings, plants, animals, and humans, wherever there is life. St. Thomas, again following the ancient tradition, distinguishes three biological powers: nutrition, growth, and reproduction. The power of nutrition serves to preserve the existence of the individual, the power of growth causes the individual to develop, and the power of reproduction ensures the preservation of species. These three basic biological powers are common to plants, animals, and humans.

St. Thomas raises an important and difficult question here, one that reappears throughout the course of the history of philosophy and is, moreover, often improperly understood. Where is the boundary, first of all, between the presence and absence of life and, next, between the presence and absence of knowledge? Experientially, as I said before, these boundaries are extremely elusive and difficult to establish. Today, for example, thanks to scientific research, we know far more than our predecessors about viruses and other such things, and this should help us determine the boundary between the living and the nonliving world. Nevertheless, the question still persists. Philosophy asserts with complete confidence that there is a boundary between the living and the nonliving, but opinions concerning exactly how and where this boundary lies will continue to vary along with the advancement of the particular sciences.

Panvitalistic philosophies (from *pan*, meaning "all," and *vita*, meaning "life"), which have their origin mainly in Platonism, reject all sharp boundaries between living and nonliving things. They maintain that everything is alive—that the whole seemingly nonliving world is permeated with life. St. Thomas disagrees. He says that there is a distinct boundary between life and the absence of life. When we call something a plant, we are saying that it belongs to the first group of animate beings, the group in which we find the functioning of exclusively biological powers—nourishment, growth, and reproduction—but no knowledge in the strict sense of the term. Biologists and other natural scientists have puzzled over whether plants are capable of knowledge. No doubt certain plants do have a kind of quasi-knowledge, just as, for example, certain minerals, though essentially devoid of life, may be said to have a kind of quasi-life (it is "as though" they were alive). Ultimately, the boundaries between both the presence and absence of life and the presence and absence of knowledge are empirically inaccessible to us. They cannot be determined experientially.

It is very significant that for St. Thomas the boundary between knowledge and the absence of knowledge occurs between the plant and animal world, and not between the animal and human world. Animals belong to the great family of knowing beings. The reason this is so significant is that in modern philosophy we see a sharp departure from this view beginning with Descartes, who maintained that animals are mere mechanisms, remarkable wound-up machines. Knowledge does not appear until we reach the world of human beings; in animals there is no knowledge. St. Thomas takes a completely different view. Animals, he says, are related to humans not only because they are living beings but also because they are cognitive beings. As we saw earlier, the principle of life in a living being is its substantial form, its fashioning element, and we call this element the soul. Thomas speaks without hesitation of plant souls, animal souls, and human souls. Whatever has life has a soul.

Thus, wherever there is life, there the fashioning element, the substantial form, is a soul. And, in turn, wherever the soul, or substantial form, has the kind of nature that can be enriched or enhanced by other forms, by other fashioning elements, there is knowledge. Three passages from St. Thomas will help us better understand the essence of what is meant by knowledge. In knowledge there is always a knower and something known. It make no difference whether this knower is a very primitive animal, a highly developed animal, a human being, or an angel. There is always a subject that does the knowing and an object that is known. Knowledge occurs when some aspect of the object passes into the knower, something that enriches the knower. Knowledge is basically, therefore, a process whereby the knower is inwardly enriched.

Here is how St. Thomas puts it: *Cognoscentia a non cognoscentibus in hoc distinguuntur quia non cognoscentia nihil habent, nisi formam suam tantum; sed cognoscens natum est habere formam etiam rei alterius. Nam species cogniti est in cognoscente. Unde manifestum est quod natura rei non cognoscentis est magis coarctata et limitata. Natura autem rerum cognoscentium habet majorem amplitudinem et extensionem. Propter quod dicit Philosophus quod anima est quodammodo omnia* (*ST* I, 14, 1). We have here one of those wonderful, classic texts of St. Thomas. He says that a being with the power of knowledge differs from a being without the power of knowledge in that the latter has no form but its own (its fashioning form), whereas the former is by nature capable of having—*natum est habere*—the forms of other things. Hence, it is clear that the nature of a thing incapable of knowledge is more *coarctata* —more restricted and limited, and that the nature of a being capable of knowledge has a greater amplitude and extension. Therefore, the *Philosophus*, i.e., Aristotle, says that in human beings the soul is everything in a way— *anima est quodammodo omnia.*

The last words are a famous saying of Aristotle. Why is the human soul "everything in a way"? Because we can know everything; we are enriched by everything that becomes an object of our knowledge. Hence, the soul in a certain sense becomes everything. Whether we know a cloud, the structure of an atom, or a wonderful work of art, we are enriched by it all; all of it enters into us, so to speak. According to St. Thomas, the determining factor in a being's capacity for knowledge is its form. The more this fashioning factor, this form, the soul, predominates over the material factor and the more the body is fashioned by and subject to the fashioning factor, the more capable of knowledge a being becomes. Thus, the more the formal, fashioning factor prevails over the material factor, the greater a being's potential for knowledge.

Continuing on, St. Thomas writes: *Plantae non cognoscunt propter suam materialitatem*—plants do not know, because of their materiality. They are incapable of knowledge because their form, their soul, is too immersed in the matter and does not prevail over it. Soon we will discuss sensory knowledge. Animals and humans have senses. A sensory power is capable of knowledge because *sensus autem cognoscitivus est quia receptivus est specierum sine materia, et intellectus adhuc magis cognoscitivus, quia magis separatus est a materia et immixtus... Unde, cum Deus sit in summo immaterialitatis... sequitur quod ipse sit in summo cognitionis* (*ST* I, 14, 1). A difficult concept appears in this text, one that needs a few words of explanation, namely, the concept of *species*, which I shall render here as "cognitive form." In the process of knowledge, there is an intermediate factor between the knower and the known object that causes the known object to be able to be in some way taken in by the knowing subject. It is precisely this third factor, which in technical Scholastic terminology is called *species*, something "like" an object, that the knower knows. If I look at this briefcase, the *species* of the briefcase enters into me, as it were.

We should not take this to mean that there is some third object between this briefcase and me, which is in some way able to enter my eyes or my mind. There is no third thing. The *species* is an aspect; it is this briefcase as seen by me, as conceived by me. To see, of course, means one thing, and to conceive, another. We will be discussing the difference between sensory knowledge and conceptual knowledge. The *species* is not some sort of object that hovers between the known object and the knowing subject. Rather, it is a kind of apprehension, a kind of aspect, which, in technical language, is called the formal object. I can never know this briefcase in its entirety, through and through. Whatever we know, we know "aspectively," only from a certain aspect or side. Whether we see, hear, or conceive, these are all aspective apprehensions, and it is in this sense that the concept of *species* is used in the passage cited above.

Next, St. Thomas discusses how these aspects of things reveal themselves to us: *Sensus autem cognoscitivus est, quia receptivus est specierum sine materia*—a sensory power knows because it receives the aspects of things without the matter. This material briefcase does not enter into me or into my eyes; rather, I receive a certain aspect of it, a certain image. *Et intellectus adhuc magis cognoscitivus, quia magis separatus est a materia et immixtus*—and the intellect is even more capable of knowing because it is even more separated from and unmixed with matter. From this St. Thomas derives a further conclusion: *Unde cum Deus sit in summo immaterialitatis, sequitur quod ipse sit in summo cognitionis*— since God is immaterial to the highest degree, it follows that God must be *in summo cognitionis*—a knower in the highest degree. God is completely immaterial, because God is an absolutely noncomposite spirit. Even pure spirits are composed of essence and existence, but God is simply existence.

Thus, the degree of a being's ability to know increases in direct proportion to how immaterial it is, that is, in direct proportion to the degree in which the immaterial principle, the fashioning form, prevails over the material principle. In plants, matter is still so unsubdued that the soul does not arrive at the level of knowledge. In animals, there is already sensory knowledge, and, in humans, intellectual knowledge as well. Pure spirits have even a higher capacity for knowledge, and in God knowledge reaches its absolute maximum.

In all knowledge, therefore, the determining factor is a being's fashioning principle, its form. We know from our previous reflections that matter cannot exist without form, because matter is pure potentiality, and potentiality cannot exist by itself. Matter alone, matter not fashioned by form, would be a contradictory being. If such a contradictory object like matter without form could exist, then it would be, as St. Thomas says, absolutely unknowable.

In modern philosophical thought, one frequently encounters the view that we, in our knowledge, can apprehend sensory images or concepts but not things themselves. St. Thomas is a realist in his theory of knowledge, which means that he maintains we really know things. When I look at this briefcase, it is not merely an image of the briefcase that I know but the briefcase itself, though only certain aspects of it. I never know anything completely. Only God has such profound knowledge of everything; we do not. Our knowledge, whether it be in the sensory order or in the intellectual, spiritual order, is always only aspective knowledge. In any case, all knowledge, both in animals and in humans, takes place where the formal factor, the soul, prevails over the material factor, the body, to such a degree that the soul is able to go out from the body, so to speak, and unite with other objects and be enriched by new forms, by the aspects of things around it. Knowledge is always an enrichment of the knower. This tenet is a central feature of St. Thomas' whole teaching on knowledge.

17

The External Senses

In the works of St. Thomas, we encounter a very distinctive approach to the problem of knowledge. Unlike many modern philosophers, who view the theory of knowledge as philosophy's main concern and tend to treat it as a separate discipline, Thomas does not present us with a critique of knowledge. What we are about to consider, in seeking to understand St. Thomas' views, is his philosophy of knowledge, his attempt to grasp the very mechanism of human knowledge. What does it mean to know? How do the different stages of knowledge proceed? These are the kinds of questions we shall be considering. We are not concerned here with the various aspects of knowledge that are subject to scientific observation and experimentation, but with its ultimate causes.

But, one might ask, why are we beginning with knowledge, and not with conduct or creativity? The order of considering these three areas of human activity—an order St. Thomas adopts from the ancient classical tradition —is by no means accidental. Thomas, like every realistic philosopher, wants his thought to be in accord with the nature of things, and this requires the priority of *logos* over *ethos*, that is, the priority of the cognitive sphere over the behavioral sphere. This does not mean that behavior is inferior to knowledge or that knowledge always precedes behavior in time. The primacy in question here is one of nature. Knowledge is prior in nature. Priority belongs to it by nature because we must first know in order to act. This is an important principle, one that in modern European thought was, unfortunately, often abandoned. Every utilitarianism, every approach that puts usefulness before truth (*utilitas* in Latin means "utility"), reverses this order. *Ethos*, the behavioral sphere, then takes precedence over *logos*, the cognitive sphere, and this subverts the nature of things. Goethe was well aware of the significance of this conflict. In *Faust*, Mephistopheles does a parody on the Prologue to the Gospel of St. John, where it is said: *In the beginning was the Word*. The Word here is knowledge, a manifestation of the most perfect self-knowledge in the Trinity. Rather than consent to the primacy of the Word, the devil proposes to Faust: *In the beginning was the deed.*[14] The evil spirit here becomes an advocate for the denial of the priority of *logos* over *ethos*, which leads to far-reaching and dangerous consequences.

We should also bear in mind that the realm of truth is not less important than the realm of love. They are of equal value. When St. Paul, in the famous passage from chapter 13 of his First Letter to the Corinthians, says that love is greater and emphasizes its endurance, he is speaking of an entirely different matter. He is referring to the fact that love is the one virtue that endures unchanged throughout eternity. When, however, it is a question of worth, then the realm of truth is just as important as the realm of love. In the Eastern rite, after the reading of the Gospel, we hear this marvelous invocation: *sophia*—the Greek word for wisdom. This is an expression of the importance of the realm of truth, which reaches its culmination point in the Gospel.

We need to keep these general presuppositions in mind as we proceed now to a more detailed analysis of knowledge, beginning with a discussion of St. Thomas' view of the vast cognitive sphere of sensory knowledge.

Leaving aside God's knowledge, which we considered when we discussed the attributes of God, St. Thomas speaks of three types of knowledge with which creatures are endowed. These are the types of knowledge found in animals, humans, and angels. In this life, human knowledge can never be of the angelic type. Angelism is a great danger, one to which Neoplatonic philosophy is particularly susceptible. Human knowledge is simply human. Our knowledge has a great deal in common with the kind of knowledge animals have (it would be interesting to do a comparison of St. Thomas' views on this topic with those of contemporary authors). An animal's knowledge may in many ways surpass our own, and yet it is always of a lower category because it does not go beyond sensory knowledge. Sensory knowledge is the kind of knowledge we have in common with animals, but it occurs in one way in us and in another in animals.

St. Thomas strongly emphasizes the psychosomatic unity of the human being, who, like all other beings, with the exception of God, is composed of two elements, potential and realization. In us, our body is the potential factor and our soul the realization. Our soul weaves our whole personality, our whole nature, from the lowest aspects to the highest. The unity of these two components is so strong that in the order of existence, or, as we say today, in the existential order, it never happens that only one type of knowledge is realized in us in isolation. When we receive the lowest form of sensory impressions, these impressions in some way involve our entire psyche. There are no really isolated sensory impressions. Consequently, when we focus here on a certain kind of sensory or rational knowledge, this should not be interpreted to mean that it occurs in a pure form. An awareness of the psychosomatic unity of the human being is important for pedagogical reasons, for it can help educators better understand those whom they are educating.

In every life activity, however great or small, the whole human being is expressed. Father Jacek Woroniecki, OP, once said that there is no experience, even the most sublime mystical experience, that does not have reverberations in our whole personality—in our intellectual, sensory, and biological spheres. There are purely spiritual experiences, but they are so in their nature and not in the way they take place. In our actual experiences in this world, our whole being always comes into play. At times this fact is falsely interpreted by psychologists, who, lacking a philosophical foundation, conclude that there are no really distinct powers in us, no really distinct types of knowledge or activity. They are inclined to believe with St. Augustine that, since there is only one human soul, there are no distinct powers, but only different manifestations of that one soul.

From the fact, however, that our whole being comes into play in each of our cognitive activities, it does not follow that we do not have a variety of really distinct powers and levels of powers. Similarly, just because the metaphysical elements of composite beings—ourselves and other creatures—cannot be dissected and "put in a jar," it does not follow that such beings are not really composed of those elements. Although it is impossible to separate potential from realization and place the body alongside the soul, yet they are really distinct.

In keeping with the ancient Aristotelian tradition, which during the medieval period was further developed by the Arabian philosophers, St. Thomas accepts a multiplicity of sensory powers in the human being. The natural sciences, it should be noted, were then being developed primarily by physicians; medicine was the area in which the experimental sciences evolved. The sensory powers are distinguished by the fact that they always operate through a bodily organ. They perform all of their cognitive activities through the mediation of empirically observable organs. We will return to this point when we examine the rational, spiritual powers of the human being. In this life, our rational powers are also dependent on the functioning of sensory powers, but they do not operate through a bodily organ. In contrast, every sensory power operates always through a concrete bodily organ. This is why the sensory powers are said to be organic.

Our cognitive powers differ from one another. St. Thomas determines their number and type based on their respective objects. Thus, the different objects of knowledge also indicate different cognitive powers. In keeping with the commonly accepted tradition, St. Thomas distinguishes two groups of sensory powers: the external senses and the internal senses.

The external senses are the familiar five senses—sight, hearing, taste, smell, and touch. Today, of course, in experimental psychology, medicine, physiology, and biology, many more external senses are enumerated beyond these five basic ones. A great many subordinate senses are differentiated. For example, the sense of touch is seen to include the sense of balance, temperature, space, etc. The ancient Greek philosopher Democritus, the founder of atomism, explained the mechanism of sensory knowledge by means of a theory of tiny images or miniatures of things. He said that every object sends out multitudes of images of itself. Knowledge takes place when these images enter our sensory organs, causing us to perceive the object. If Democritus were right and our knowledge really were to take place by means of wandering miniatures, then knowledge would have to occur according to the principle of like by like. In other words, we would know those things that found their way into us. For example, a certain color that we know, a certain colored patch, would have to enter into us in order for us to be able to perceive it. Such were originally the naive ways in which sensory perception was understood. The eye would have to be colored by the hues it sees; the ear, the organ of hearing, would have to contain the sounds it hears; and so on.

St. Thomas presents an interesting opposing view, which even today finds adherents among natural scientists. He says that a sensory organ that receives a certain sensation must lack those qualities it perceives. In order for us to experience taste, our taste buds cannot already be "tasty"; they must be completely devoid of such qualities in order to be able to actually perceive them. Likewise, our organ of sight must itself be devoid of colored qualities in order to be able to perceive, or cognitively receive, colored patches. In general, then, a sensory organ must be completely devoid of all the essential properties of its proper object in order to perceive them. This principle will play an important role in Thomas' attempt to demonstrate the unlimited nature of our spiritual powers.

Each of the five external senses has its own proper object, adapted to its own particular cognitive abilities. Here we must be very precise. The sense of sight does not know things, the sense of hearing does not know melodies, etc. For this, as we shall see, other powers are needed. The sense of sight knows colors; only colors are the proper object suited to sight. The sense of hearing knows particular sounds; only sounds are the proper object suited to hearing. Stated generally, the external senses have as their proper objects particular sensory qualities—colors, sounds, flavors, odors, etc.—and not things. This is an important principle because, as we shall see, it establishes the need for the indispensable role played by the internal senses. An awareness of this role, along with knowledge about the human being supplied by biology, psychology, and other sciences, can help facilitate communication among people, especially the kind of communication that requires an acquaintance with the internal structure of the human being.

St. Thomas sees a certain gradation among the senses. This does not mean that he regards some senses as more dignified or refined than others. For St. Thomas, the lowest is just as worthy of respect as the highest. We have already drawn attention to his respect for even the smallest, most insignificant things. The gradation he introduces here has to do with a certain hierarchy. According to St. Thomas, the most basic and decisive sense for the human personality is the sense of touch. This is the sense that determines whether we are "thin-skinned" or "thick-skinned" (Thomas borrows these descriptions from Aristotle). This has implications for our intellectual life. The subtlety of our sense of touch in some way affects our intellectual life. The other senses, in hierarchical order, are taste, smell, hearing, and sight. Sight is regarded as closest to the intellectual sphere, although for certain people hearing may become a much more "intellectual" sense than sight.

St. Thomas also addresses the problem of sensory illusions, a topic of interest to psychologists and philosophers alike. One of the points of departure in Descartes' philosophy was the fact that, in our knowledge, we are susceptible to illusions, especially when estimating distances, locations, etc. St. Thomas states very definitively that *non decipitur [sensus] circa obiectum proprium* (*ST* I, 17, 2, ad 2)—a sensory power never errs with respect to its proper object. Hearing never errs with respect to sounds, or sight with respect to colors. Errors occur only in our judgments. Only when we begin to reflect upon what our senses are conveying to us and begin to make judgments about our impressions can errors and illusions arise. That is what St. Thomas is saying in these words from the *Summa*.

The sphere of the external senses is the most fundamental cognitive sphere in both humans and animals. If we were deprived of all our sensory powers (which would be impossible in this life), then we would have no rational life at all. This does not mean that our rational life takes place through our sensory organs, i.e., through the mediation of something bodily, but rather that it is dependent upon and arises genetically from the data we gather through our sensory impressions. Consequently, it is extremely important that we cultivate and develop our sensory knowledge and become adept in this rudimentary area, the realm of the functioning of these most elementary external senses. But—and this bears repeating—if these external senses were the only cognitive powers we possessed, our knowledge would not extend beyond the perception of disconnected colors, sounds, tastes, etc. We would not know, sense, or experience any objects, any multiplicity of things in the world. We would live in a chaos of sensory qualities. There would be nothing more in our consciousness.

18

The Internal Senses

In order to know things, to distinguish the multiplicity and variety of objects around us, and to react properly to different stimuli, we need a whole group of internal senses. This is where the significance of the physiological-philosophical theory of the internal senses comes to light. Modern psychology has all but forgotten this theory, but it was highly developed in the ancient and medieval tradition. Like the external senses, the internal senses are organic powers, that is, they operate through organs. From its inception, this tradition proclaimed the organ of the internal senses to be the brain, the central nerve organ, both in humans and in animals. St. Thomas and his contemporaries would have rejected the notion that the brain is the organ of thought. The brain is the organ of the internal senses, whereas thinking—cognitive intellectual activity—is inorganic. This is how St. Thomas viewed the matter.

This is an important point, one generally overlooked and not appreciated in the sometimes rather simplistic discussions that take place between spiritualists and materialists on these issues. The organs of the internal senses are more or less precisely localized portions of the brain. The determination of where these organs are located in the brain also has a long tradition, based not, as is frequently charged, on pure speculation but on a large number of experiments, often horrifying in their cruelty. After Aristotle's death, his school moved first from Athens to the island of Rhodes, and then to Alexandria. There, under the reign of Ptolemy and other Egyptian rulers, it developed into one of the best schools of antiquity and also amassed an extensive library. In this scientific research institution, which was called the Museion (because it was intended as a shrine dedicated to the muses, whence the name "museum"), many important scientific investigations were carried out.

There hundreds of people were condemned to vivisection at the hands of physicians seeking to understand the nervous system. Science advanced at the expense of human misery. People were tortured in order to discover the workings of the central nervous organ and the peripheral sensory organs. These experiments, which continued for over a century, were supplemented by numerous observations of the wounded and of people whose brains had been exposed in one way or another. As can be seen, research on localizing the organs of the internal senses in the areas of the brain was already being carried out early on. Also, in Krakow and elsewhere, some interesting sketches have survived from medieval times, especially from the late medieval era, depicting attempts to localize the internal senses in specific areas of the brain.

An understanding of the cognitive sphere of the internal senses is vital for an understanding of the functioning of the human personality. St. Thomas' doctrine protects us both from materialism and from pseudospiritualism, because it not only acknowledges the importance and superiority of the spiritual functions but it also reflects a deep appreciation for the fundamental worth of sensory knowledge. There is a famous remark by Spinoza (no doubt aimed at St. Thomas and all empiricists who regard the senses as the basis of knowledge), who said scornfully: the Scholastics proceed from material things, Descartes from the human self, and I from God.[15] He conceived of God in a pantheistic way and carried the pantheistic view to its zenith. In contrast, we find in St. Thomas an attitude of total respect for the lowliest material dimension of reality. All of our knowledge has its source in sensory experience, and so it is important to understand the extremely complex structure of sensory knowledge.

The investigations I mentioned above, which in the days of antiquity were concentrated mainly in Alexandria, were continued by the later medical tradition. Two of the most famous names connected with this tradition in the Middle Ages were the Greek physician Galen (2nd c.) and the Arabian physician and philosopher Avicenna (10th c.). This tradition flourished in the great medieval medical schools, especially in Salerno, not far from Naples, and in Montpellier, in southern France. These are very interesting matters historically. Medicine was then an extremely important science. Apart from medicine, there was no experimental biology, physiology, or psychology. Medicine was virtually the core of the natural sciences. St. Thomas also relies on the results of the medical investigations of his day and, in keeping with this tradition, accepts four organic internal sensory powers, whose organs are different parts of the brain. Of course, these localizations were very general. They were not as precise as they are today, but they are still very interesting and illuminating.

The most basic internal sense is the common sense (*sensus communis*). This is the power that performs as though the central role, gathering together the perceptions received through the mediation of the external senses. If this internal common sense did not exist, it would be absolutely impossible for us to coordinate the perceptions received through the individual external senses, and we would not be able to refer these perceptions to objects. It is only thanks to the common sense that we can speak of the sensory perception of objects. The common sense allows us to join together the sounds, tactile sensations, flavors, odors, etc. proceeding from some single source and refer to the object that is the real source of all of these impressions. To compensate for their lack of intellectual powers, some animals have much more highly developed external and internal senses than humans. In us the intellectual cognitive powers in a certain way weaken the intensity of the perceptions of the external senses and the functioning of the internal senses.

The common sense, says St. Thomas, is also the sensory power that allows us to become aware of an experienced perception. If this sense did not exist, we would be recipients of those same disconnected sensory qualities, but without being conscious of it. St. Thomas describes the role of the common sense in a succinct, characteristic text: *Unde oportet ad sensum communem pertinere discretionis iudicium, ad quem referantur, sicut ad communem terminum, omnes apprehensiones sensuum; a quo etiam percipiantur actiones sensuum, sicut cum aliquis videt se videre* (*ST* I, 78, 4, ad 2)—we must attribute to the common sense a *discretionis iudicium*, a certain discriminating judgment, a designating, evaluating, ordering judgment, to which, as to a common term, all the perceptions of the external senses must be referred. Only this kind of judgment, executed by the common sense, allows us to distinguish and classify perceptions. I look at this table, but it is thanks to the common sense that I am able to distinguish all the objects, all the wholes of what I see, hear, touch, etc. The common sense is that by which *percipiantur actiones sensuum*—by which we are aware of the activity of the external senses, such as, for example, that we see that we see (*videt se videre*). If there were no common sense, then neither animals nor humans would be conscious of their sensory perceptions.

The second internal sense is the passive memory (*imaginatio sive phantasia*). The Latin term *imaginatio* has nothing in common with the way we use the term "imagination" today. *Imaginatio* is derived from *imagines*, which are the images or phantasma that are stored up and retained in the subject experiencing sensory perceptions. We do not store disconnected impressions of qualities, but images produced by the common sense. The passive memory is a treasury or storehouse of images, of sensory perceptions joined into wholes. These groups of perceptions that have been united by the common sense are preserved in us; they do not vanish without a trace. The passive memory allows us not only to preserve memories but also to apprehend structural wholes. If we had no memory, we could neither hear a melody nor see a picture, a landscape, or a scene. Strictly speaking, when, for example, we look at a beautiful stained-glass window, we never apprehend the whole picture at once, but we must somehow successively traverse the elements of the picture and put them all together. For this we need both the common sense and memory, in order to join these elements into a whole and to remember that they refer to the same object. The same is true of hearing a musical phrase. When we begin to hear a melody, if we did not have the passive memory and the common sense, we could not even grasp the simplest whole, a few melodic bars, much less the whole musical composition.

The third internal sense is the active memory (it has two Latin names: *memoria* and *reminiscentia*). Whereas the passive memory is the ability to retain impressions and images, the active memory is the ability to recall or extract them and bring them to light at our bidding. St. Thomas and his contemporaries believed that animals also have an active memory, but animals do not activate this memory dependent on need as we do. For an animal to remember something, certain stimuli are necessary, whereas we can remember at will. We ourselves are sufficiently active to be able to actualize this treasury of ours and extract from it the images we need at any given moment. This is why St. Thomas calls the active memory in animals *memoria* and in humans *reminiscentia*. The difference between the two is that memory in animals is actualized only as a result of an external stimulus, whereas reminiscence in humans is actualized at the bidding of the subject doing the remembering. We have an active memory that is, as it were, fully developed. Moreover, from freely selected elements in this—figuratively speaking—treasury of memory, we can create new groups. This is the power of creative imagination, which can operate either in an aimless fashion or in a very purposeful way. When employed with a purpose in view, it serves as the basis of all creative human endeavors. Consequently, the creation of a work of art is not merely an intellectual activity, but also involves the use of the active memory and the imagination (referred to above as the passive memory).

The most valuable and important internal sense in the life of both humans and animals is instinct (*vis aestimativa*, the estimative sense). This is a significantly higher power of judgment than the common sense. The common sense makes judgments by carrying out a kind of segregation and classification; out of a haze of sensory qualities it forms a whole, organizing them according to established types. Something else is at issue in the case of instinct. It judges the usefulness or harmfulness of certain perceptions for the perceiving subject. This highest organic sensory power, which is called *vis aestimativa* in animals and *vis cogitativa* in humans, is localized in the central part of the brain. In animals this instinct, or estimative power, is absolutely perfect and unerring. In us, because of the proximity of the spiritual cognitive powers and, says St. Thomas—speaking here as a theologian—because of the disturbance in these intellectual powers as a result of original sin, the functioning of this estimative power has also been disturbed. Our instinct, as we know only too well, is much less perfect than that of animals, and so we are forced to rely on our intellect. But the human intellect, unfortunately, is not as it once was, as possessed by our first parents before sin. Our instinct, too, our *vis cogitativa*, is usually underdeveloped, existing as though only in embryonic form. Animals, by virtue of their estimative power, act unerringly. They know *hic et nunc*—in any given time, place, or circumstance—what is absolutely necessary for them. They select exactly the objects they need. We see this absolute purposefulness and flawlessness everywhere—in the migration of birds and fish, in the building of nests by birds and the construction of damns by beavers. The same applies to the things animals avoid. Instinct gives them the invaluable ability to discriminate between what is beneficial and harmful.

Among human beings, the proficiency of instinct increases the closer they are to nature, the less over-intellectualized they are, and the more they live in harmony with their natural environment. People who live in the forest, at sea, or on the great expanses of the African continent definitely have a far more highly developed instinct than we deteriorated city dwellers.

The *vis cogitativa* is such an excellent sensory power that St. Thomas does not hesitate to call it *ratio particularis*, particular reason. The greatness of our intellect consists in the fact that we can do something animals cannot, namely, form concepts, but concepts are always general, even though they can apply to individuals. The *vis cogitativa*, on the other hand, allows us to attain the most perfect knowledge humanly possible of individual, concrete beings. Consequently, *ratio particularis*, particular reason, is a fitting name for this power; it is reason, but reason in reference to absolutely individual objects. Today, especially among Thomists, this power is once again beginning to be investigated and appreciated. Why? Because in philosophy the understanding of existence is such a central issue (I am thinking here of the Lublin School of Philosophy, and particularly of Mieczyslaw A. Krapiec, OP), and what exists is always concrete. Detached universals do not exist; only particular beings exist. And particular reason, *ratio particularis*, is one of the ways in which we come in contact with concretely existing, particular beings.

To distinguish the perfect instinct of animals from the weakened, deteriorated, often declining instinct of humans, animal instinct is called *vis aestimativa*, and human instinct *vis cogitativa*. The word *cogitatio* calls to mind thinking, suggesting a connection with the sphere of thought, whereas *aestimo*, which means "I estimate," indicates that this is a power that, in the case of animals, unerringly appraises what is advantageous and disadvantageous.

The fact that all of these senses are more perfectly and fully developed in animals than in us is yet another important reason to respect the animal world. From the above analysis, we can also see how crucial the sphere of sensation is, for it serves as the foundation of our whole spiritual life— not just our natural spiritual life but also, indirectly, our supernatural life as well. We are dealing here with the base. Just as, in the realm of the external senses, the sense of touch is the foundation and the other senses are in some way constructed upon it, in the same way the internal and external senses together constitute the indispensable and vital substructure of our whole conscious life.

19

Rational Knowledge

All beings that are endowed with knowledge, from the lowest to the highest, including the whole world of pure spirits—apart from God, in whom absolute unity reigns—are equipped with two types of activity. One is cognitive activity and the other is concupiscent or appetitive activity. The words "concupiscent" and "appetitive" should not be understood here in the sense of lustful or sensual; that is not what is at issue. Knowledge and desire appear in humans in both the sensory and the rational sphere. Here we are concerned with the rational, spiritual activity proper to human beings. It is important not to confuse the spiritual and the supernatural. Here we are considering only the natural spiritual plane. According to St. Thomas, we are endowed with a form of knowledge that is rational, inorganic, and essentially different from sensory knowledge. It is the highest knowledge accessible to us in the natural order, and, in a certain way, it brings us into proximity with the world of pure spirits.

Among the ways in which rational knowledge has been understood, there are basically two views. According to one, our rational knowledge is spiritual and inorganic and does not operate through a bodily organ. The external senses each have their particular organs, the organs of hearing, smell, etc., and the internal senses have theirs, the brain, the central organ of the nervous system. Rational knowledge is inorganic and not dependent on sensory knowledge; it takes place independently of what the senses convey to us. The other view, which St. Thomas represents, maintains that rational knowledge is inorganic in its essence, and so it does not operate through a bodily organ, but it is dependent on sensory knowledge. In our condition here on earth, sensory knowledge is a precondition of rational knowledge.

The first view is found among proponents of anthropological dualism, those who conceive the human being in a dualistic fashion. They picture the soul as "sitting" in a kind of hermetic bodily container; the soul is not connected in an organic, profound, internal way with matter. The soul and the body are two completely independent things, joined in a merely accidental way. As we know, St. Thomas takes just the opposite view. The soul and the body are intimately connected with one another, and only together do they constitute a human being. This also leads St. Thomas to adopt the second view of knowledge.

Our rational knowledge never comes to us ready made. This is a very important point. We do not receive ready-made concepts, judgments, or arguments. Instead, we must work them out for ourselves and arrive at the content of our rational knowledge on our own. Our rational knowledge is essentially different from the kind of knowledge possessed by God. God, as pure realization, pure act, comprehends everything through and through. God sees absolutely everything without having to go through the trouble of arriving at this knowledge. We, on the other hand, are in potentiality with respect to the knowledge of everything, and we must arrive at this knowledge by passing from potentiality to realization. This leads to a further point. Our rational knowledge, according to St. Thomas, requires two rational cognitive powers.

In the philosophical language used by St. Thomas, a rational cognitive power is called an intellect. Contrary to what is sometimes said, St. Thomas speaks explicitly of two rational cognitive powers. Because there is potency and act (the realization of this potency), St. Thomas, following the ancient Aristotelian tradition, says that there is an *intellectus in potentia*, a potential intellect, and an *intellectus in actu*, an *intellectus agens*, a realized intellect. The terms "passive intellect" and "active intellect," which are sometimes used to denote these two powers, do not express what is at issue here. The potential intellect and the realized intellect are not two aspects of a single power. In St. Thomas they are two really distinct intellectual cognitive powers.

If we were to gather together all the discussions and debates that have concentrated on this point over the course of the history of European thought, we would end up with an impressive library. The reason this issue was so hotly debated, discussed, and investigated was that it held the key to the entire difference between St. Thomas' view of knowledge and that of the Platonists and, later, the Augustinians. In comparison to God, or even to angels, our rational knowledge is extremely weak and imperfect. St. Thomas says that we possess just the first glimmerings and seeds of rational knowledge. Although our rational knowledge is so very imperfect, it is nevertheless of enormous worth, because it is a sign of that spiritual aspect within us that qualitatively distinguishes us from the rest of the animal world to which we belong.

In discussing the concept of the human being with those who subscribe to a materialistic philosophy, we must be very careful that the subject of the debate is clearly defined and understood in the same way by both sides. It follows from St. Thomas' view of knowledge that we must receive all our cognitive data through the senses. We are incapable of knowing anything spiritual directly. This means, for example, that no one has ever seen God. St. Thomas completely agrees with this revealed truth. Here again we have a *revelabile*—an agreement of philosophy with revelation. It also means that we have no direct intellectual access to anything real, including spiritual beings. This is an important principle for our inner life.

Borrowing an ancient metaphor, St. Thomas says that, at the beginning of our rational life, our intellect—both the potential and the active—is a clean blank slate, a *tabula rasa*. The perceptions that enter our consciousness by way of the external senses and are changed into images by the internal senses are alone what allow us to make entries on this blank slate. We do not come into the world already equipped with a set of concepts or ideas. St. Thomas here disagrees with Plato. According to Plato, the human soul exists before conception and is more or less randomly assigned to the body in which it exists. When the soul enters the body, it brings with it a "package" of concepts that it came to know in the other world. These concepts make up the actual content of the soul's spiritual life. St. Thomas rejects the notion that we have any innate ideas or concepts. We must work at acquiring all our concepts, from the moment we experience our first childhood perceptions until the day we die.

As we have seen, every cognitive power has its own proper object suitable to it. The proper object of sight is color, that of hearing is sound, etc. In the same way, the intellect must have an object proper to itself. According to St. Thomas, the object suited to every intellect—divine, angelic, and human—is being in general, everything that exists. In the case of the human intellect, however, this object is finite. The human intellect is limited to the knowledge of material things. Thus, material things in general, or, as we say in technical language, the natures of material things, are the proper object of the human intellect. This is important because, as we shall see, it forms the basis upon which St. Thomas establishes the immateriality of our intellect.

We noted earlier that if our organ of sight were actually colored we could not see colors, and if sounds were sounding in our organ of hearing we would not be able to hear anything. A given organ must itself be devoid of that which is the essential quality of its proper object. Likewise, if material things in general are the adequate object proper to the human intellect, then, in order to be able to know them, the intellect must itself be devoid of matter. This is the essence of St. Thomas' argument for the immateriality of the intellect. Anyone who rejects the thesis that material beings are the proper object of the human intellect will also reject St. Thomas' reasoning and conclusion here. This argument for the immateriality of the intellect works only in the context of a view of knowledge such as St. Thomas advances. This view of knowledge, in turn, seems to be the most legitimate one because it expresses the truth about the human being more realistically and more in keeping with the objective state of affairs than the Platonic or Augustinian view.

We know material beings with our senses, and we can also know them with our mind. When I look at this tape recorder, touch it, listen to it, etc., I get different sensory images of it. These tactile, auditory, and visual images are all located in the sensory sphere. In addition to these images, however, on the basis of my many years of experience, I form a concept of a tape recorder by virtue of which I know what a tape recorder is in general. This concept of a tape recorder is a product of my intellect, whereas the image of a tape recorder is a product of my senses. I form the concept out of the whole variety of images I have received, experienced, and absorbed by my sensory memory. In order to go from an image to a concept, I need rational cognitive powers: a potential intellect and an active intellect.

The fact that we do not stop at the level of images but are able to go on to form concepts is very significant. Concepts allow us to communicate with one another by means of articulated, fully developed speech, in contrast to the vocalizations used by animals. Animals also have a language of their own by which they in some way convey their images. We, however, are able to communicate our concepts through various signs and transpositions of those signs, which together make up our articulated speech, that is, language in which we operate with parts of speech, sentences, etc. A comparison of animal and human speech reveals both the great difference between the sensory and the rational spheres as well as their profound connection. To understand why St. Thomas maintains that there are two intellectual powers in us, a potential intellect and an active —realized—intellect, we must explore the spirit of his empiricism, which has as its basic tenet that we derive all our knowledge, all our cognitive material, from the senses and transform it into spiritual content.

Here is an important text from the *Summa Theologiae*: *Intellectus... humanus qui est infimus in ordine intellectuum et maxime remotus a perfectione divini intellectus, est in potentia respectu intelligibilium, et in principio est sicut tabula rasa, in qua nihil est scriptum... quod manifeste apparet ex hoc quod in principio sumus intelligentes solum in potentia, postmodum autem efficimur intelligentes in actu* (I, 79, 2). This is a fundamental text; it summarizes what we have been talking about. *Intellectus humanus*—the human intellect—*est infimus in ordine intellectuum*—is the lowest in the order of intellects. We have already seen that the angelic intellect is far superior to the human intellect and that the fewer concepts a spiritual being needs to use in order to know, the more perfect it is. We ourselves need an enormous amount of concepts for knowledge to take place, whereas God needs only the Word, which is identical with God. The human intellect is, therefore, the farthest removed from the perfection of the divine intellect. *Est in potentia respectu intelligibilium. Intelligibilia* are objects of rational knowledge. Our intellect is in potency with respect to all objects of rational knowledge. *In principio*—in the beginning (this can be understood as either the beginning of life or the beginning of the different cognitive processes)—*est sicut tabula rasa in qua nihil est scriptum*—it is like a slate upon which nothing has yet been written. In the beginning, *sumus intelligentes solum in potentia*—we are rational knowers merely in potency, and only later do we become rational knowers *in actu*—do we realize our concepts.

This famous text is a wonderful summary of the basic ideas we have been considering. I once belonged to a group that spent a whole year reading St. Thomas' *De Veritate*, which is a magnificent reflection on the question of truth. Thomas says there that we have in us *conceptiones universales*—general schemata or apprehensions. Without them, as the contemporary structuralists would say, a small child could not learn to speak at all. These *conceptiones universales* are not innate ideas or concepts, but schemata, which are somehow activated and begin to operate as soon as they come in contact with the data collected by the senses. Sometimes this statement of St. Thomas is interpreted in a Platonic-Augustinian spirit. But here there is no reference to innate concepts; all that is innate are the schemata that St. Thomas calls *conceptiones universales*.

The process of rational knowledge, in which both the potential and the active intellect play a role, takes place, according to St. Thomas, in more or less the following manner: Sensory images, the images we obtain as a result of sensory knowledge, are received by the potential intellect. In order, however, for a concept to arise out of the images of, for example, a tape recorder, these images must be suitably illuminated and transformed. The illuminating agent, our inner light—which, of course, like everything else, operates thanks to the light of God—is the *parvum lumen*, the tiny light of the active intellect (*intellectus agens*). As a result of this illumination, the images are transformed into concepts. The active intellect, however, like the schemata mentioned above, would be unable to operate were it not aroused by the data collected by the senses. St. Thomas stresses here that the intellect is not and cannot be an organic power.

If this is how rational knowledge takes place, then it is absurd to say that the brain is the organ of the intellect. The brain is the organ of the internal senses. The intellect, in contrast, is inorganic. It cannot be an organic power, a power that operates through a bodily organ, if it has all material beings as its proper object. Let us recall that a cognizing organ must itself lack what it cognizes. If the intellect were to have an organ devoid of matter, this organ would be a contradictory object, because matter is part of the very concept of an organ. This is an argument that is not mentioned at all today because it is thought to be obsolete and connected with an antiquated biology or physiology. In reality, however, it has nothing in common with any of the natural sciences, because the natural sciences explain the world in their own way, and the analysis presented above is of a distinctly philosophical nature. Hence, the value of this argument remains intact despite the changes that have occurred in the natural sciences.

Consequently, neither of our intellects are or can be organic, bodily powers. They are essentially different from our sensory cognitive powers, even though, as we have seen, if we had no sensory cognitive powers, these intellects could not operate in us at all in our earthly human state (later we shall discuss how differently St. Thomas thinks our knowledge will look in our eschatological state). If, therefore, our potential intellect, the intellect that receives information, is by nature immaterial, then it cannot receive spatiotemporal images. These images must be dematerialized and spiritualized in order for our potential intellect to be able to receive them. The power that effects this transformation of the images is precisely the *parvum lumen*, the little light that is our active intellect.

For an image to be transformed into a concept, it must be dematerialized and generalized. This process of converting images into concepts is called abstraction. To speak abstractly, therefore, does not mean to talk about nonexistent, fictional things. One often hears it said that we think abstractly when we are not concerned with this world, when we do not have our feet on the ground, but have our head in the clouds. This has nothing to do with abstraction in the philosophical sense. *Abstraho* in Latin means "I detach," "I separate." To abstract means to separate out from images everything in them that is spatiotemporal and to cull from them their common content, a concept. When we are in a group and look at the people around us, we each have as many images of human beings as there are people in the group. Something different happens when we form the concept of a human being. This concept is what we abstract from the images of the people we have met over the course of our lives. The concept of a human being is something fundamentally different from the thousands or even millions of human images that reside in our sensory memory. The process of going from images to concepts takes place by means of abstraction. The agent responsible for this transformation is the active intellect, following which the potential intellect—to use St. Thomas' description—"gives birth" within itself to a concept.

Let us consider another beautiful text: *Contemplatio humana secundum statum praesentis vitae non potest esse absque phantasmatibus... sed tamen intellectualis cognitio non consistit in ipsis phantasmatibus, sed in eis contemplatur puritatem intelligibilis veritatis* (*ST* II–II, 180, 5, ad 2). Perhaps no one can express a thought so incredibly succinctly and concisely as St. Thomas. In this he is unrivaled among the Scholastic masters. Human contemplation in our earthly state of life (*statum praesentis vitae*) cannot take place without images. There is no contemplation without an image. Contemplation without images is a fiction. No matter how much we retire from the world, we will never attain such contemplation. Our contemplation, however, does not consist in images alone (*non consistit in ipsis phantasmatibus*), but in them we contemplate the purity of spiritual truth (*sed in eis contemplatur puritatem intelligibilis veritatis*). This text is wonderful also because it shows how even the purest spiritual activity in our present state is connected with sensory determinants. The full accompaniment of the activity of our sensory powers is with us as long as we live, which in no way diminishes the immateriality and inorganic nature of our intellect. Lack of a proper understanding of the nature of the intellect, its proper object, and how it differs from the internal senses is a main cause of the serious misunderstandings that arise in discussions on these topics between materialists and those who maintain the immateriality of the human soul and human intellect.

20

Cognitive Realism

What distinguishes us from animals is the fact that we can go beyond sensory knowledge; we can go from images to concepts, to articulated speech, and to all that results from this. What results is culture, the whole of human creativity, so different from animal creativity. Though the creativity of animals may in many respects even surpass our own, it differs from our creativity in that it never changes or develops. It lacks the unlimited evolution we see in human creatively. Human speech and culture continually change and evolve.

On the other hand, a great deal also differentiates us from pure spirits. It seems strange that St. Thomas, who places such a strong emphasis on empiricism, on the experiential basis of all human knowledge and activity, nevertheless speaks of the knowledge proper to angels. After all, we have no reports of how angels live, act, or converse with each other. And yet St. Thomas writes at great length and very informatively on this topic.

In reflecting on the cognitive activity of pure spirits, St. Thomas says that this is precisely where the Platonic view is applicable. An angel receives full-blown concepts from other angels and from God, just as we receive sensory images from our surrounding world. These concepts or ideas are infused into the angelic mind; an angel does not have to produce them. In other words, unlike us, an angel does not have to go through the trouble of abstraction. Angelic knowledge is not abstractive but intuitive. Here again we come upon a term whose meaning needs explanation. Intuition is not a premonition of something about to happen. *Intueor* means "I look at," "I see." Intuitive knowledge is simply knowledge that arises from viewing or contemplating. Angels have intuitive knowledge. They gaze at the concepts infused into their minds, concepts that come from God or from other pure spirits. This is angelic speech. It involves no judgments or reasoning but merely the transmission of wonderfully potent intellectual content from one spirit to another. The spiritual life of angels is, therefore, completely different from our own. Just as we cannot imagine the kind of time in which pure spirits dwell (angelic time, which is different from ours, is called *aeuum*; only God is completely beyond time), so, too, we cannot imagine what the speech of angels is like. We can speak of it as St. Thomas does, but this is far from having an image of it, and we always live and think by means of images.

Memory and the skills of memory play an important role in human life. When we discussed the internal senses, we saw that we have both a passive and an active sensory memory, which allow us to store and recall images. St. Thomas says that we also have a rational memory, which allows us to store and recall concepts. We do not constantly have to produce each concept anew. We also do not constantly have to be recreating our language; we simply have it. We have a storehouse of concepts, along with nouns, verbs, adjectives, and other parts of speech corresponding to these concepts. In this rational, spiritual memory, says St. Thomas, the aspect of the past is absent. By this he means that when we call upon our rational memory we do not reach back to something that was, but we reach instead into a present, timeless treasury, so to speak. Through the use of memory and abstraction, we are able to develop our knowledge. In contrast to angels, who receive truth by direct infusion and see it spiritually, we have to work at arriving at truth ourselves.

How do we arrive at truth? We have three kinds of rational cognitive activity, three operations of the mind.

The first rational activity consists in forming concepts and dwelling upon them. This dwelling upon the spiritual content of our concepts is the first step to contemplation. We simply pause and gaze upon the content of a concept. This attentive gazing is very complex because it encompasses a whole array of extremely rich spiritual realms. In a sense, it is a distant reflection of angelic knowledge. We have here in this first activity that which in Latin is called a *simplex apprehensio*, a simple apprehension of content. It arises directly upon the formation of concepts.

The second activity is more complex. Once we have concepts, we then connect them with one another. To join one concept to another is to form a judgment. These judgments, or propositions, have either a positive or a negative content, depending upon whether we assert that something is or is not thus and so. We also make existential judgments, in which we affirm that something exists. Existential judgments are extremely important with respect to the question of existence, especially in the matter of coming to know existence. *Ratio particularis*, or *vis cogitativa* (the internal sense of particular reason), and existential judgments are the two possible ways, one sensory and the other rational, of arriving at knowledge of existence.

The third and most complex rational cognitive activity is reasoning, the process of joining together judgments. From reasons we derive conclusions according to the various principles of logic.

European culture, which is basically Mediterranean, developed mainly as a result of the blossoming of this third activity. We have neglected the first and second and have developed the third—based on Euclid's *Elements* (geometry) and Aristotle's syllogistics (logic)—to an extraordinary degree. Although we have built an otherwise impressive culture, we have neglected the sphere of wisdom, which develops mainly in contemplation and judgment. This is a very important matter for anyone involved with the training and education of children. Professor Mieczyslaw Gogacz has made what seems to me to be an important and valuable observation in this regard. He says that in our pedagogical system we neglect the contemplative side of children and their ability to reflect philosophically, which sees its greatest development in four- and five-year-olds. The whole emphasis in our educational process is placed on the development of the rational age, the age of six or seven, when the skills of reasoning begin to evolve.

Because we live in such a mathematically and technologically oriented culture, we tend to educate children only in the spirit of the third function —reasoning. And yet the most important spiritual changes take place in children at the age of four or five, when they ask the most perplexing, most philosophical questions about the world around them. This is a decisive period for children, and the spirit of contemplation, not of reasoning, prevails in them. Our neglect of this philosophical age and concentration on the rational age is one of the greatest pedagogical mistakes of our culture. This needs to be changed and corrected, and a good understanding of St. Thomas' thought can go a long way in helping to turn this situation around.

To arrive at a proper understanding of St. Thomas' thought in this regard, we shall first have to examine how he uses three terms that frequently appear in his works. Although we often tend to use these terms interchangeably, we really should not do so, because each of them means something different. These are the terms "mind," "intellect," and "reason." By "mind" we should understand the entire realm of our spiritual powers, both cognitive and appetitive, encompassing both the intellect and the will. "Intellect" refers to the mind's cognitive powers, the active and the passive intellect. When the intellect performs the third function, the function of reasoning, it is called "reason." "Mind," therefore, is the broader concept, and "intellect" the narrower. The reasoning intellect—or reason, for short—does not form concepts or judgments but simply reasons. And in this sense, taken in the spirit of St. Thomas, we should preach a return to intellectualism and a rejection of extreme rationalism. This is a very important matter, as far as our whole approach to education is concerned. The pedagogical consequences of these attitudes are far-reaching. They are also not irrelevant for our philosophy, theology, worldview, inner life —and even prayer life.

It is not a matter of indifference whether we are idealists or realists. A cognitive realist is someone who is convinced that we are able to know the visible reality around us, and that all this knowledge is based on sensory knowledge. This is a very humanizing attitude. St. Thomas is definitely a realist. He says that we are dependent upon our surrounding reality. Although we possess the innate schemata mentioned earlier, these are schemata that do not impose anything. They merely help us better receive what reality radiates toward us. We are dependent upon this reality, but we are also capable of coming into cognitive contact with everything around us. This is the basis of all communication. We are not solitary islands. We are connected by nature with all that surrounds us, not just with other people but with the whole material world, and this material world opens up for us perspectives on the world of spirit and, most importantly, on God.

The thesis that our only way of coming into contact with reality is through the senses is the hallmark of empiricism. Empiricism, let us recall, consists primarily in the rejection of the existence of innate concepts and in the insistence that we can know nothing in isolation from the senses. Even when we receive supernatural inspirations, these inspirations always operate through our nature, which is a psychosomatic nature, one that is both spiritual and corporeal. We have no direct knowledge of God, of pure spirits, or even of ourselves. St. Thomas says that we do not know ourselves directly but only through our functions or activities, which are both sensory and spiritual. Thus, we know ourselves always only indirectly, through the acts that point to us as the subject of those acts. We do not have direct knowledge even of the first metaphysical, theoretical, or practical principles; they are revealed to us only in the course of our reflections and activities.

This is why St. Thomas does not accept the theory of illumination, or universal enlightenment, in the sense spoken of by St. Augustine. The great Bishop of Hippo appeals to the words from the Prologue of the Gospel of St. John, where it is written that there is a true light that enlightens every person who comes into the world. According to Augustine, this enlightenment would be universal and natural, which means that it would be indispensable for any kind of knowledge. Such would be the direct intervention of illumination. St. Thomas, in contrast, does not abolish or rule out the activity of secondary causes. According to him, the light within us is the active intellect, although, of course, the moving force behind everything is God, and the divine light is the ultimate cause of everything. In his commentary on Psalm 4, which makes reference to this divine light ("O Lord, let the light of your countenance shine upon us"), St. Thomas says: *Per ipsam sigillationem divini luminis in nobis omnia demonstrantur*—through this imprint of divine light in us, everything is revealed to us. But this divine light always operates through the mediation of the active intellect, that *parvum lumen* within us.

And so in our present state the body is far from an impediment to knowledge, since *principium nostrae cognitionis est a sensu*—the source of all our knowledge is in the senses. This is also true of our knowledge of God. St. Thomas addresses this point in a beautiful passage from the *Summa Contra Gentiles* (3, 47): *Cognitio Dei quae ex mente humana accipi potest non excedit illud genus cognitionis quod ex sensibilibus sumitur, cum et ipsa anima de seipsa cognoscat quid est per hoc quod naturas intelligit sensibilium*—the knowledge of God that can be attained by the human mind does not go beyond the kind of knowledge that comes from things known by the senses, since even this mind itself is able to know what it is itself only through knowing the natures of things perceived by the senses. It follows, therefore, that we are able to have knowledge of our own knowledge not directly but only through the world of material things. This is a strong statement. Among theories of knowledge and views of how it arises, St. Thomas' cognitive realism bears a certain resemblance to materialistic realism, although it also clearly surpasses it.

If this is how our knowledge as a whole looks, then it would be a mistake to think that our knowledge in the next world will be merely a higher degree of the knowledge accessible to us on earth—as was maintained by Neoplatonism and many other schools of thought. For St. Thomas, who as a theologian interprets the texts of the New Testament, including those passages in which St. Paul speaks of the future glory that awaits us, there is no doubt that the knowledge belonging to the redeemed infinitely sur-

passes our natural cognitive capabilities. What awaits us as real participants in the glory of God, and what St. Paul describes in the words, *I
shall know even as I am known* (1 Cor. 13:12), is something so great that
it requires a whole new spiritual power. This new power, this new "third
intellect," so to speak, is called by St. Thomas the *lumen gloriae*, the light
of glory. This is not merely an enhancement of our natural intellects, but a
completely new spiritual cognitive power. Without it we would not be in a
state to get even the tiniest glimpse of God face to face. This is a wonderful perspective, and only against this background can we get a sense of the
greatness and magnitude of what awaits us and to which we are called,
and which infinitely transcends even the cognitive capabilities of angels.
Lumen gloriae—this is something that allows us to know God in an infinitely better way because it is a real participation in God's own nature.

The doctrine of the *lumen gloriae*, so very characteristic of St. Thomas,
is directly opposed to the view that in our spiritual life we merely pass
through degrees, and that the highest degree of mystical experience here
on earth is already an actual foretaste of what is to come in glory. According to St. Thomas, what awaits us in heaven must be essentially different
from what we are capable of experiencing here, because, although our
entire nature is wonderful, in the order of nature we are on the lowest level
of spirit. St. Thomas' debate with the Franciscan schools had one of its
culmination points at this very juncture. In the 15th century, it was commonly believed that natural mysticism is transformed into the actual future
life, which was viewed as a development and enhancement of our present
natural life. Nicholas of Cusa is very close to St. Thomas in emphasizing
the gulf between our present and future powers of knowing God and what
God is. This gulf can be crossed only by a real participation in glory.
Without such participation, which takes place in the order of grace, this
transition is impossible. Only those who are redeemed will be endowed
with this *lumen gloriae*. For those who do not have it, this is already a
terrible fall, and for those who do, it surpasses anything we can imagine.
It was his theological interpretation of the texts of St. Paul that led St.
Thomas to this philosophical understanding of these issues. The perspective with which he presents us is marvelous, little known, and extremely
simple.

21

Conduct and Creativity

The distinction between the spheres of knowledge and activity applies to beings that are animate and conscious. In all living beings that have at least a trace of knowledge—i.e., in animals, humans, and angels, and also in God, though in a more perfect and more complete way—along with knowledge we also find the tendency to realize aims. In technical language, this tendency is called *appetitus*, appetite. The word "appetite" here is not used in its current sense but is simply a designation for all purposeful tendencies other than purely cognitive ones. In us these tendencies to realize aims occur on two different planes and constitute two separate realms. One is the realm of human behavior (*ethos*), the area of concern to ethics, which investigates how we should conduct ourselves in life, what we should strive for, and how we should act. The other is the realm of human creativity (*ars*, *techne*), the realm in which we produce works of art and in which our realized aim is a product.

At the basis of all these tendencies, both those having to do with conduct and those having to do with creativity, lies the desire or tendency called *appetitus*. According to St. Thomas, this *appetitus* (from *appetere*, "to tend toward something") is something very universal. All beings, including those that exist below the level of life and are merely inanimate bodies, display a tendency toward something. They have an *appetitus naturalis*, a natural tendency to realize their nature and to actualize all the potentiality that lies within that nature.

This tendency manifests itself differently in different beings, depending on the type of knowledge proper to them. In the world of plants and inanimate beings, which have no knowledge of their own, this tendency is unconscious; it manifests itself as the realization of God's knowledge with respect to them. On the other hand, where we find, in addition to the knowledge God has of them, beings that have knowledge of their own, as is the case with animals, humans, and angels, this tendency is conscious. In animals, we find only sensory tendencies, which are common to animals and humans alike. In humans, however, we also find tendencies connected with the will. Animals do not have a will. Humans are the only creatures

on earth with a will. In humans, therefore, there are two types of tendencies, a sensory appetite and a rational appetite. Angels, in turn, because
they are pure spirits, have only a rational appetite, only a will. An awareness of this is important for understanding the operation of all the appetitive powers, both in ourselves as well as in other beings.

The chart on the following page may be of assistance here. It is so
arranged that the most basic spheres, the lowest levels, appear at the very
bottom, and then we ascend to increasingly more perfect powers, activities, and functions. In the sphere of sensory knowledge, we have the external
senses and then the internal senses, listed according to increasing degrees
of perfection. Among the internal senses, we have the common sense,
passive memory, active memory, and instinct (i.e., *vis cogitativa*, the
power of sensory judgment in animals). These sensory powers serve as a
basis and accompaniment for all the rational cognitive functions performed by the potential and active intellect. The intellect, in turn, performs
three basic functions: it forms concepts, makes judgments, and reasons.
These functions can be directed either toward knowledge itself, and then
the intellect operates as the theoretical intellect, or toward action, and then
it operates as the practical intellect.

Something analogous occurs in the case of tendencies. The terms
"appetite" and "sensual" should not be understood here in the ethical
sense. The emotions constitute the sphere of sensual tendencies in us. Our
sensory, or emotional, appetite serves as the basis and accompaniment—
as the raw material, so to speak—for our rational appetite, which is the
will. Just as the intellect makes use of the entire sensory cognitive sphere
for its purposes, so, too, the will should make use of and control the emotional sphere, the sphere of the appetite that is a relatively sensual tendency in us. Hence, it is extremely important for us to become familiar
with how our emotions function and to conduct ourselves properly in relation
to this whole aspect of our nature.

With respect to decisions of the will, that is, with respect to determina-
tions of the spiritual appetite, the emotions perform a role similar to that
of sensory knowledge with respect to intellectual knowledge. We frequently
come across interpretations of St. Thomas' thought that deprecate the
emotions and treat them as unimportant. This is a serious misrepresentation of his view. Just as it cannot be said that St. Thomas regarded sensory knowledge as unimportant, it also cannot be said that he underrated
the emotions. St. Thomas does, however, throw new light on the ancient

debate concerning the emotions, which had its origin in two schools, the Aristotelian school and the later Stoic school.

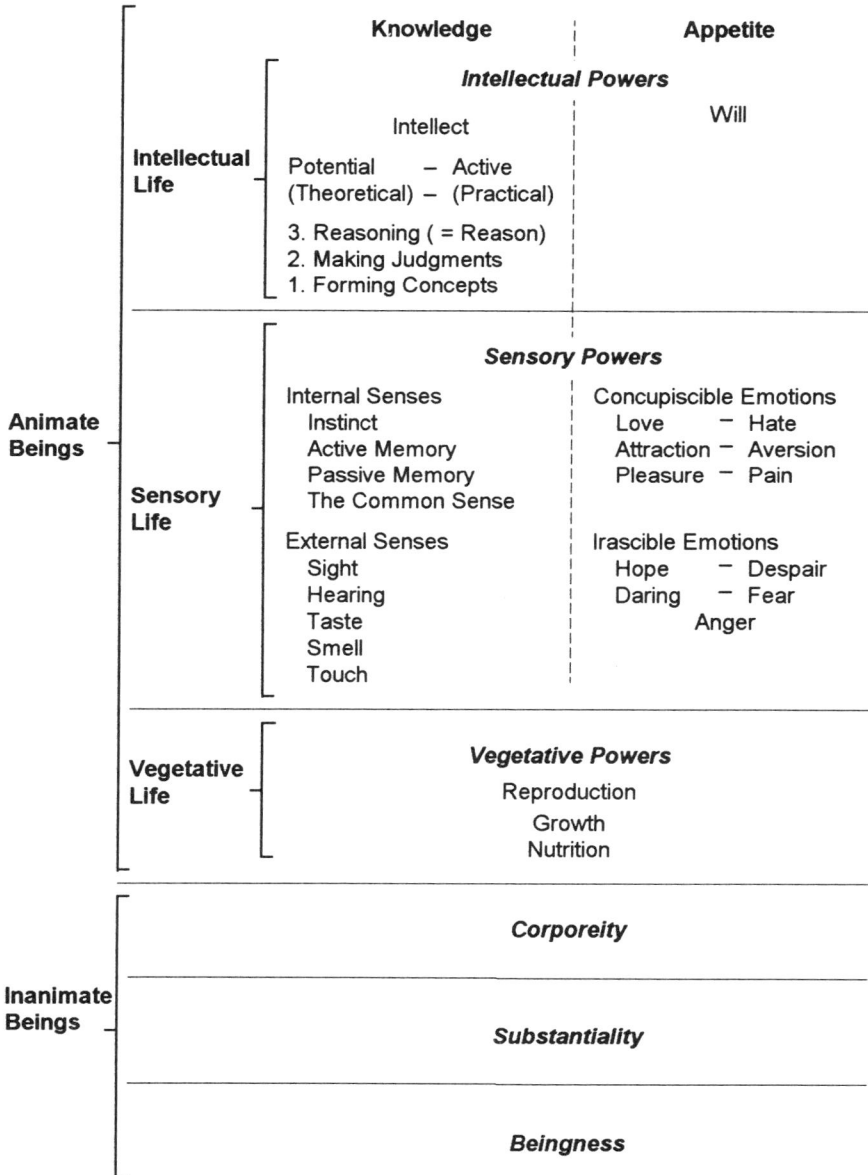

	Knowledge	Appetite
Intellectual Life	***Intellectual Powers*** Intellect Potential — Active (Theoretical) — (Practical) 3. Reasoning (= Reason) 2. Making Judgments 1. Forming Concepts	Will

Sensory Life	***Sensory Powers***
	
	Internal Senses
	  Instinct
	  Active Memory
	  Passive Memory
	  The Common Sense
	
	External Senses
	  Sight
	  Hearing
	  Taste
	  Smell
	  Touch
		Concupiscible Emotions
		  Love — Hate
		  Attraction — Aversion
		  Pleasure — Pain
		
		Irascible Emotions
		  Hope — Despair
		  Daring — Fear
		  Anger

Vegetative Life	***Vegetative Powers*** Reproduction Growth Nutrition	

Animate Beings brackets the Intellectual, Sensory, and Vegetative Life.

Inanimate Beings

Corporeity

Substantiality

Beingness

The Aristotelians and Stoics disagreed on the meaning, role, and value of the emotions. For the Stoics, the ideal person, the wise person, was the emotionless person, one who was able to suppress all emotion. Such a person was characterized by *apatheia* (the Greek term *pathein* means to be passive, to undergo emotions, and *a-patheia* means to be without emotion). The Aristotelians very strongly opposed the Stoic view. They said that we should by no means be emotionless, but we should properly train our emotions. St. Thomas here follows the Aristotelian line completely, and so to give his view of the human being a Stoic interpretation, and even to go so far as to say that he was an enemy of the emotions, is an erroneous portrayal of his thought. St. Thomas' concern was to understand the nature and function of the emotions in the context of the extremely rich and mysterious whole that the human being is.

The only sense in which it might be said that St. Thomas devalues the emotions is that he would not agree with the practice that arose some centuries later, more or less since the time of Kant, near the end of the 18th century, of speaking of reason, will, and emotion all in the same breath, as three similarly rational, spiritual powers in us. St. Thomas does not place the emotions in the rational sphere, and in this sense he may be said to devalue the emotions. It is quite common to hear the phrase "reason, will, emotion" bandied about. St. Thomas, in contrast, maintains that we have only two rational, spiritual powers: intellect (with the qualification that we have both a potential and an active intellect) and will. The emotions, despite all their importance, are located in the sensory sphere. From an educational point of view, it is important to be aware of where the emotions arise and what role they play in our psychological life. The whole vortex of desires, feelings, and sensations are under the sway of the emotions and are located in the nonrational, nonintellectual part of our being, the part we have in common with animals. In us, however, this part should be governed by the will, enlightened by the intellect. If we fail to exercise control over this sphere by our will and intellect, we run the risk of allowing our emotions to become the guiding factors in our lives, in our conduct, and in our creativity, and this is morally harmful and wrong.

As we can see, the emotions are unquestionably an important part of us, just as sensory knowledge is. The fact that we have them in common with animals is yet another reason for treating animals with understanding and compassion, since animals (especially the more highly developed ones) are not mere machines but beings with an extremely rich emotional and sensory cognitive life. Already in Plato, Aristotle's mentor, we find the notion that the main task of all education is to gain control over this wild and unruly vortex of emotions, not just so that they will not harm us, but so that they will cooperate as much as possible in the ultimate realization of our goals. And this, as we shall see, is where the virtues come in.

Of course, the virtues deal directly not with the emotions but with acts of will, and yet ultimately these acts of will operate on this great psychological vortex of emotions. Plato's works contain numerous images that speak to this truth, including the famous image of the two horses in the *Phaedrus*. One of these horses is very skittish and stubborn, while the other races ahead splendidly and submissively. Together they symbolize the uncontrolled, unruly, emotional part of us, over which we gradually gain control with our intellect and, above all, with our will. An Aristotelian motif appears here, one that we find emphasized even more strongly in St. Thomas. The intellect cannot alone properly take advantage of this vortex; the will must intervene. This is an anti-Stoic stance. It aims at a vibrant emotional life. It does not seek to extinguish or destroy the emotions, but to use of them in every way possible and to subject them completely to our spiritual side, that is, to the will directed by the intellect.

We have two kinds of emotions. This is a motif that St. Thomas also adopted from the ancient philosophical-medical tradition. In this tradition, the emotions are seen as divided into two great realms. One is the realm of emotions that are appetitive in the strict sense of the term (the concupiscible emotions, *concupiscibilitas*), and the other is the realm of the irascible emotions (*irascibilitas*, from *ira*, meaning "anger"). All of these emotions, both of these realms, let us always remember, belong to animals as well. The strictly appetitive emotions, those in the first realm, aim at securing the things we need. The irascible emotions, in turn, help us to overcome all obstacles and to undertake struggles and difficulties in order to achieve the various goods toward which the appetitive emotions direct us. All higher animals are endowed with these two types of emotions, and we, too, possess a rich supply of them.

In the appetitive sphere, St. Thomas enumerates three pairs of opposing emotions: love—hate, attraction—aversion, and pleasure—pain.

When it comes to the theory of love, hardly anyone has written more profusely and profoundly on this topic than St. Thomas. According to Thomas, love has its origins in our psychological life as an emotion arising from attraction. Plato was right, therefore, when he said that love is born of beauty. In order for love to begin, we must be aware of the beauty of the beloved object. One of the most wonderful philosophical and literary texts of all times is the famous speech of Diotima in Plato's *Symposium*. Diotima, an emissary of heaven, comes to Socrates and explains what true love is. This is really an exceptionally beautiful text. It so impressed certain 12th- and 15th-century Christian authors that they said Socrates was surely a saint, a naturally holy Christian. Erasmus of Rotterdam even invoked him with the words: *St. Socrates, pray for us.*[16] According to Diotima, love begins from the love of what is beautiful in a completely external way, and then slowly, by degrees, moves from the external to the more internal, from the love of what is beautiful to the eyes to the love of what is beautiful to the spirit, ultimately arriving at beauty itself. And here Diotima directly asserts that God is beauty without any imperfection, total beauty, without even the slightest trace of ugliness.

Love always presupposes a knowledge of what is loved. The higher our knowledge, the truer and deeper becomes our love. Knowledge that just skims the surface allows us to be attracted to and love external things, and knowledge that reaches deep within allows us truly to love what is within. St. Thomas says that love, which is always originally and at its root an emotion, becomes true love to the degree that it is transformed into an act of will. In this way, emotional love turns into spiritual love. Different authors have described this as the sublimation of the emotions. The emotions, which are themselves sensory, are transformed into something spiritual by being taken up by the will and included in its act. The will is not meant to extinguish the emotions but to sublimate them, subjecting them completely to higher ends. To the degree that we manage to do this, our emotions are mature. But since we never accomplish this completely in the course of our lives, we always remain somewhat emotionally immature. This is a great developmental task that endures our whole life long.

St. Thomas' view of the relationship between love and knowledge is both interesting and beautiful. Love is always dependent upon a prior knowledge. I must know what I love. But there need not be a direct proportion between this knowledge and love. St. Thomas says that we can love perfectly something that we do not at all know perfectly. He gives two examples of this, one from the natural and one from the supernatural order. His example from the natural order is the love of knowledge. When we begin to learn something, we do not know what we are about to learn, but we would not even attempt to learn it if we did not love what we want to know. From the supernatural order, he uses the example of the love of God. We can never know God in a perfect way, but there is no limit to how much we can love God. Knowledge must precede love, since knowledge is the foundation of love, but there does not have to be a proportional relationship here.

St. Thomas goes deeply and extensively into the subject of love. Here we are considering only certain aspects of his treatment. The first is his thesis that there need not be a proportion between knowledge and love; the second concerns his distinction between two types of love.

One type of love consists in the tendency to fill up the lacks we perceive in ourselves. We know that we are lacking in many things, and we love those who are able to fill up these lacks. This is love of the lowest order, the love of concupiscence (*amor concupiscentiae*). It is always, even if very nobly conceived, a tendency toward our own benefit, toward the satisfaction of our own needs. In true love, we do not seek to satisfy our own needs but to enter into communion with the one we love and to be truly united with that person, not thinking of whether it will bring us some advantage. This is a union that leads to the realization of increasingly greater goods. St. Thomas, christianizing and significantly deepening Aristotle's thought in this regard, calls such love the love of friendship (*amor amicitiae*). This is no longer the love of yearning, the love of concupiscence, the tendency to satisfy our own needs, but the love that seeks a common good in friendship.

The love of friendship is the prototype of love, whereas the love of concupiscence is on a lower level and is, so to speak, merely a prelude to spiritual love. With this in mind, St. Thomas says that going out from oneself is an essential property of love. Every love—not just mystical love —is ecstatic in this sense, since *extasis* means "to go out from oneself." Our love and longing for the good increase and the egocentricity that binds us to the love of concupiscence decreases in direct proportion to our ability to look beyond ourselves and to forget ourselves. Consequently, those philosophical schools that accentuate the importance and primacy of turning toward the subject, toward ourselves, and also those schools of spiritual life that focus mainly on perfecting our own souls rather than on contemplating the ultimate object of our desire, namely, God, are susceptible to the danger of descending to the lower level of love. True love is the love of friendship.

The most profound utterances concerning purely spiritual love in no way encourage us to sever its ties with the emotions. Spiritual love is not love from which the emotions have been eradicated. Earlier we saw that in the cognitive sphere, even in the highest acts of mystical knowledge, the sensory realm must always play a role. This is also true in the appetitive sphere. I want to emphasize that there is nothing wrong with describing love as an emotion, so long as we remember that such love is the lowest, most primitive expression of love. In us, such love should be transformed into an act of will; sensory love should become spiritual love.

We should also remember that every emotion has a contrary, and the contrary of love is hate. *Omne odium ex amore causatur*—all hate is caused by love (*ST* I–II, 29, 2). Hate is the reverse side of an unsatisfied, imperfect, disordered love. It arises when what we love does not live up to our expectations. We often have only ourselves to blame for this. It usually results from our failure to discern the true state of the object of our love, which leads us, in turn, to overrate it and regard it too highly.

Once on television there was an extremely interesting short film about wild dogs in the bush. It was a documentary about the social life of a pack of dogs, and in it one could clearly see the emotions at work. It showed a poor mother dog being tormented by dogs from another family. They eventually forced her to leave the pack, and all her pups perished. The program showed exactly how the events transpired. Love and hate, anger and jealously—the whole wild vortex of emotions was clearly in evidence. Because animals lack an intellectual superstructure, they are governed in the emotional realm, as in the cognitive realm, by raw instinct, which in some sense takes the place in them of intellect. Sometimes their instinct substitutes for intellect in a very efficient way as far as the good of the species is concerned, but it also always operates in a pitiless way, with no concern for the good of an individual in conflict with the group.

Love and hate sometimes assume a very basic, rudimentary form, and they develop into the even more primitive emotional responses of attraction and aversion. This pair of emotions is, in turn, subject to the still more basic emotional attitudes of pleasure and pain. This third pair of concupiscible emotions is the deepest and most primitive.

In St. Thomas we find a naturalism, which can also be called a realism. It finds expression in his belief that whatever is an essential element of a nature—in this case, human nature—is good in itself. This is a consequence of the metaphysical principle that everything that exists is good; nothing is positively evil. In keeping with this orientation, St. Thomas rejects a view of the emotions that came down from antiquity to the

Middle Ages by way of Cicero. Cicero called the emotions diseases of the soul. In this context, St. Thomas' treatment of the emotion of pleasure, and particularly of the role that this very basic emotion plays, is extremely interesting.

The emotions as such are morally neutral. Their goodness or badness depends on how they are used. The value of the pleasurable emotions is determined by the value of the love with which they are associated. According to St. Thomas, pleasure is entirely good provided that it is ordered to an end, but it must never become the sole motive of conduct and an end in itself. St. Thomas devoted a separate treatise to an investigation of the topic of angels in order thereby to bring human nature into clearer relief. Similarly, in the course of examining the problem of original sin, he reflected on the subject of pleasure. He raises the question of how Adam functioned in the state of innocence, and of how human life would look if there had been no original sin and if our will and intellect had not become disordered. In developing these reflections, he makes an amazing statement, one that may also serve as a rejoinder to every type of angelism and Puritanism: *Fuisset tanto maior delectatio sensibilis quanto esset purior natura et corpus magis sensibile* (*ST* I, 98, 2, ad 3)—the pleasure in the sensory sphere would have been greater to the extent that the nature was purer and the body more sensitive.

One might think that a person who lived so ascetic and disciplined a life as Thomas would scorn the sphere of sensory pleasures. Instead, just the opposite is true. He says that self-denial has value only when we know what we are giving up. This implies that what we consciously give up should be something of real value, and not just "scraps and remnants." St. Thomas links the value of the feeling of pleasure in the state of innocence to the fact that human nature was then purer and the body more sensitive. He thus introduces the notion of so-called "thin-skinned" people. We are all "thick-skinned" because original sin operates in us. A person without original sin would be sensitive and subtle—in short, "thin-skinned." This consideration helps us appreciate what we have lost as a result of original sin and where we are now. It is an expression of an anti-Stoic, anti-Puritan, anti-angelistic position. We bear within us a vestige of our greatness, not just a sign of corruption. An offshoot of the emotion of pleasure is joy, whereas pain, the contrary of pleasure, is connected with sorrow.

In addition to the three basic pairs of emotions in the concupiscible sphere, St. Thomas lists five emotions in the irascible sphere. He does not subscribe here to a pattern dictated from above that would require pro-portion to reign. He is a realist. He proceeds from the observation of reality. In one sphere he lists six emotions and in the other five. This is one of the signs of his philosophical realism, for in philosophy it is easy to fall victim to the temptation of thinking that all divisions and schemas must exhibit a wonderful proportion. Based on observation, St. Thomas concludes that anger is an emotion that has no counterpart. Among the irascible emotions, which are essential to animals in their struggle for survival, there are two basic pairs, hope and despair, and daring and fear, plus the emotion of anger.

Hope is one of the most powerful forces in all behavior. We should not confuse the emotion of hope with the virtue that goes by the same name. The emotion of hope appears in both humans and animals. Daring is also not a virtue. Hope, however, does have a counterpart in the supernatural virtue of hope, whereas daring is not transformed into a virtue. The coun-terpart of daring is the virtue of fortitude, both on the natural and on the supernatural planes. Daring is an emotion. One can be daring and not have fortitude. It is often a long way from this natural daring to fortitude. Daring and fear belong to the emotions. Not until fortitude do we enter into the realm of virtue.

Anger, *ira*, is an emotion that stands alone. We know what the term IRA means today in Ireland. The very name is symbolic. *Ira* is anger, which can become a substitute for justice. Where one does not rise to the level of the virtue of justice, there anger begins to operate. It is the emo-tion that, if not properly controlled and exercised, is the one that most strongly clouds the operation of our intellect. Anger need not always be bad; sometimes it is even genuinely useful and necessary. The emotions themselves, as I said before, are ethically neutral. They are neither good nor bad. They are the strings upon which the entire melody of our ethical behavior is played. They are also the proper material of our moral life. Morality consists ultimately in allowing all our behavior to be guided by what is highest and most important in us, and in the appetitive sphere this is the will.

The will is the rational appetitive power whose task it is to make use of the whole realm of emotions and to direct our behavior and creativity. This is the area for which we are most responsible. The will should govern the emotions, but it should itself, in turn, be subject to the intellect, which apprehends the end. The will performs its task as a power if it leads us to this end and is subject to it, and if it directs our actions toward the realization of all the ends we regard as important. It is up to the intellect to discern these ends. The intellect, in discerning our ends, is operating in the sphere of wisdom. This is one of the reasons why wisdom is such an important intellectual virtue. The virtues, as we shall see, improve both the intellect as the rational cognitive power and the will as the rational appetitive power. Animals cannot be said to have virtues. Virtues appear only where there are spiritual powers—intellect and will.

Every step we take in every moment of our life should be taken as a result of a free decision of our will, or else we will end up being led by the blind tendencies of our emotions. This is an extremely important point. If we were entirely devoid of will, and if, as in the case of animals, our powers did not extend beyond the internal senses and the emotions, then we would be determined and not free. We would have to behave in a certain way. Only with the presence of free will does the sphere of freedom open up. St. Thomas says that any view that does not accept the freedom of the will is basically unphilosophical. In this sense, every determinism, in denying the freedom of the will and the freedom of decisions made by the will, is unphilosophical. The issue of the freedom of the will is a critical one for understanding the world of spirit. This world should not be confused with the supernatural world, which develops under the influence of grace. St. Thomas speaks of the natural spiritual world in which we already dwell, but in which animals and plants have no part. It is also the world of angels and, most importantly, of God.

The more our will is in harmony with our intellectual knowledge and the clearer this knowledge is, the freer we are. In God there is no discord between knowledge and will, and God's knowledge is absolutely complete, so God's freedom, too, is maximal. All of God's actions are infinitely free. God is not compelled, for example, to create anything whatsoever. The whole work of creation is a work of absolute freedom. There were those who suggested that if God had not created the world something fundamental would have changed in God. According to St. Thomas, the creation of the world does not change anything in God; the world is completely external and unnecessary in relation to God. God's external activity does not affect the internal nature of God at all.

In angels the balance of intellect and will is still imperfect, and in us this balance must constantly be achieved anew. The more our will is determined by our intellect and the less we are swayed by the vortex of our emotions, the freer we are. We achieve this freedom by becoming increasingly more spiritual. Thus, freedom turns out to be the antithesis of caprice, license, or arbitrariness. Freedom does not consist in being able to do whatever we please or whatever we want, but consists instead in constantly bringing our will into harmony with our intellect. At issue here is not the intellect as a repository of exceptional scholarly learning but the intellect as a source of wisdom. Our intellect directs us toward and points out to us the ends we ought to pursue. This explains why St. Thomas insists that the root of all freedom lies in reason.[17] By "reason," as we know, St. Thomas means the reasoning intellect, the intellect in its highest function. The determination of ends must involve some sort of practical reasoning. According to St. Thomas, then, the root of freedom lies in reason, that is, in the intellect as determining our ends. The will is a separate spiritual power, our highest power next to the intellect.

Philosophers have for centuries debated the question of whether the will or the intellect is more important. St. Thomas maintains that the intellect is more important because the will should rely on it and should follow the light of the intellect. In the beginning was the word, not the deed. The following adage is also true: *Nil volitum, quod non praecognitum*— nothing is willed that is not first known. The primacy of the *logos*, of the intellect, of the cognitive factor, is, as we have already seen, a primacy of nature. This does not mean that the will is less important, for the whole moral value of an act ultimately depends upon the will. We are responsible for our acts of will.

The will, however, is also in a certain sense determined, because there are things that we must will. St. Thomas says that we cannot not will the good. We can err with regard to particular goods, but we must will the good in general. Likewise, we cannot not will happiness. *Voluntas ex necessitate inhaereat ultimo fini, qui est beatitudo (ST I, 82, 1)*—the will of necessity adheres to the ultimate end, which is happiness. St. Thomas, following St. Augustine here, says that in seeking happiness, however we understand it, we are unwittingly seeking God, for if we had complete knowledge we would know that God alone is happiness. Consequently, our quest for happiness is an unconscious quest for God.

22

Habits: Virtues and Vices

We have already seen that the will is an appetitive power in the rational sphere, and thus it is a spiritual power. This means that the will is an inorganic power; it does not operate through any bodily organ whatsoever. As a rational power, the will exists alongside the cognitive power in the rational sphere and is intimately connected with this power, which is the intellect. We have also already seen how St. Thomas understands the freedom of the will. He is a staunch opponent of determinism, the view that regards the will as determined, necessitated, or coerced by some factor other than itself. St. Thomas subscribes to the view that is sometimes called "self-determinism." He says that the more fully the will submits to the judgment of the intellect, the freer it is. The more clearly the intellect knows the end of behavior and the more fully the will agrees with and submits to the direction of the intellect, the freer the will becomes. The will does not act in a necessary way.

At the same time, we must will happiness, and we must also will the good in general. There are, then, certain objects of desire, certain ends, that attract the will in a necessary way, but when it comes to choosing the means to these ends and making concrete decisions, the will is free. We are not governed by blind fate (*fatum*). During St. Thomas' time, there was a widely held theory that all events that take place in the world, including all human actions, are determined by the constellations of the heavenly bodies. This theory of astral determinism, which was promoted by astrologers, was also applied to religion. The emergence of a religion was thought to be dependent upon the heavenly bodies. This view, prevalent in St. Thomas' day, became even more prominent in the 14th, 15th, and 16th centuries. Thomas opposed it from the start. He said there is no fate, including astral fate. If our decisions and actions were not free, then there would be no point to morality or ethics (the theory of morality), for we would not be responsible for any of our deeds.

Another theory is that of genetic determinism, which may take a psychological or sociological form. According to this view, we are so completely determined by heredity and conditioned by our environment that we actually cease to be responsible for our actions. There is no such thing as sin, everything is excused, and no one is morally responsible for anything. In this view, morality and ethics also lose all meaning. We are determined in our decisions in a necessary way. St. Thomas presents us with a response to this difficulty: *Libertas ad actum inest voluntati in quolibet statu naturae respectu cuiuslibet obiecti* (*De Veritate* 12, 6)—freedom of action lies in the will; this freedom is connected with the essence of the will in every circumstance and with respect to every object. It is because of the will, which is in its very essence free, that we speak of human deeds. Animals, in contrast, do not perform deeds, although they do carry out conscious activities. Animals decide on the basis of emotion, and all their emotions are governed by instinct. This is how the more or less highly developed animal organisms always function.

St. Thomas analyzes human actions and, in the course of his analysis, enumerates a series of phases in them. We do not, however, experience these phases as occurring successively. They may be distinguished in analysis, but from a temporal point of view they occur simultaneously. They are completely interrelated, as are all our powers and all the acts of these powers. Here we shall consider a few of the more important phases and analyze them in a cursory way. This should help us see how closely intellectual cognitive elements are connected with determining elements (i.e., acts of will) in every human action, and how thoroughly the will is connected with the intellect.

In his analysis of human activity, St. Thomas distinguishes four basic phases:

1. Intention (*intentio*). For most medieval philosophers, especially the great Peter Abelard, a 12th-century scholar who worked in the region of France, intention was a kind of synopsis of all that could be said on the topic of human activity. For St. Thomas, in contrast, intention is the first but not the only element of our conscious acts. Every conscious act aims at an end. Intention consists in selecting the end to be pursued and in directing ourselves toward it. Consequently, intention is both an intellectual and a volitional act. It involves an intellectual apprehension of an end, as well as a tendency toward that end, for as soon as we know the end we want to pursue it. Thus, intention encompasses two factors, an intellectual cognitive factor and a volitional appetitive factor. In the phase of intention, what interests us is an end. This need not be the ultimate end, but simply the end that happens to be under consideration at a given moment.

Although happiness and the good are always the ultimate end of all our efforts, a host of intermediate ends stands always before us along the path of life. Intention, then, involves knowing the end and directing the will toward the end we have in view.

2. Deliberation (*consilium*). The second element of action pertains not to the end, but only to the means that will lead us to the end. *Non erit consilium [de fine], sed de eo quod est ad finem* (*ST* I–II, 14, 2, ad 1)— deliberation concerns not the end, but the means to the end. Here we are in the purely intellectual sphere. St. Thomas says that this phase concludes with a judgment of practical reason. The intellect here appears as reasoning and practical because it is concerned with the realm of doing (conduct) or making (creativity). This phase leads to a judgment of practical reason —or, more precisely, to several judgments, since the same end can be reached by various means. We compare and evaluate these different practical judgments. This is what it means to deliberate. Deliberation may last a whole hour or take place in the twinkling of an eye.

3. Consent (*consensus*). The third phase is an act of will. It is not yet the final act, but one in which the will simply expresses agreement with and gives consent to some of the judgments proposed in the deliberative phase. It rejects certain practical judgments as unsuitable and consents to others. It says that they may enter into the reckoning because they represent means conducive to the already selected end. *Voluntas quasi experientiam quamdam sumens de re cui inhaeret* (*ST* I–II, 15, 1)—the will, as it were, draws experiential conclusions concerning the things to which it adheres. We find ourselves here in what might be called the experiential field of the will. The previous phases were intellectual-volitional intention and intellectual-cognitive deliberation, whereas consent is purely volitional.

4. Free choice (*electio*). All of the above phases lead up to the fourth and final phase. From among the several possibilities we have accepted, from among the several practical judgments concerning possibly suitable means, we choose one of them, one of the ways that will lead to the desired end. Here, again, as in the phase of intention, St. Thomas sees such an intimate connection between the intellect and will that, in his commentary on Book VI of Aristotle's *Ethics*, he calls choice *appetitivus intellectus vel appetitus intellectivus*—appetitive intellect or intellectual appetite (VI *Ethic.* II, 5, 2). It follows from the analysis of these phases that for St. Thomas the connection between the intellect and the will is

extremely close in any of our activities that are not mere reflexes but consciously performed actions.

This, then, is how St. Thomas views the structure of human action. Moral development consists in becoming increasingly more proficient in all of these acts. These phases are very difficult to master. We may go for years without emerging from a situation, never making a conscious choice but always remaining in suspension. This is the unhealthy state called abulia, which results either from a lack of will or from a certain discord between the intellect and the will. We may, however, also reach the point of being able to go through these phases efficiently and quickly.

Moral development does not consist in simply becoming aware of what we ought to do. St. Thomas is clearly opposed to the Socratic ethic that says it is enough to think well in order to act well. It is not enough to think well; we must also repeat certain actions in order to learn how to act well. All training in morality consists in a repetition of acts. Merely telling those in our care how they ought to behave usually ends in failure. They must become accustomed to repeating the acts as fully as possible, with all the phases that occur in them. We must train those in our care—or ourselves, in developing ourselves—to repeat the acts as fully as possible, with all the phases that occur in them. If we are to perform meaningful actions, and if our lives are to be fully human and not just a series of unfinished acts, we must develop both of our powers: we must have a mature intellect and a mature will.

Herein lies the whole meaning of virtues as habits. The intellect and the will, our two spiritual powers, the one cognitive and the other appetitive, ought to be developed in a positive direction. They can also degenerate in us and develop negative habits. Virtues and vices are habits that arise in us through the repetition of acts. Father Jacek Woroniecki, one of the better known ethical theorists in the early part of this century, to whom we as young academicians in the twenties were greatly indebted, made a distinction between a reflex and an action, and also between a conditioned response and a habit. Animals can acquire conditioned responses, and the whole training of animals consists in producing such responses in them, but only humans can have habits. The whole realm of virtues and vices opens up before us here, a realm that does not exist in animals. Reflexes, which are common to both humans and animals, can be morally neutral, but there are no morally neutral human actions. Each of our actions, if it is an action, makes us more proficient in either a positive or a negative direction.

From birth to death, therefore, we are always developing, whether we like it or not. Every action makes us more proficient—unless we live beyond the realm of action in some dream-like state of reflexes and conditioned responses. Then there reigns in us an ethical neutrality, to which the following words surely apply: *neither cold nor hot* (Apoc. 3:15). Such a state is morally bad. St. Thomas says that *dispositio fit habitus, sicut puer fit vir* (*ST* I–II, 49, 2, ad 3)—just as the boy becomes a man, dispositions become habits, constantly growing stronger and more ingrained. What begins as a disposition toward some habit eventually becomes the habit itself. St. Thomas agrees with Aristotle here that a virtuous habit is not greater the more difficulty it requires, but just the opposite: the easier it is to do something, the greater the virtue in that area. According to the Stoics and Kant, difficulty belongs to the very essence of virtue. St. Thomas, in contrast, says that the point of acquiring virtuous habits is not to overcome difficulty but to make it increasingly easier for us to perform certain deeds. Art, in the broad sense, is also a virtue. A shoemaker who always finds it hard to make shoes is not a good shoemaker. This applies to all other areas as well.

Only those actions that are in keeping with the light of the intellect have the ability to transform a disposition into a virtue. Throughout this discussion, we are dealing with ethical issues in the natural order. We are still far from the order of grace. On the natural plane, then, those actions that conform to the light of the intellect are good, and those that do not conform to it are evil. They can be neutral only when they are independent of the light of the intellect—but then they are not actions at all but mere reflexes. The ordination (*ordinatio*) of an act to an end is a basic concern for St. Thomas, but it does not tell the whole story, as it does for Abelard. We saw earlier that intention is fundamental to action from a moral point of view, but it is still insufficient. Nevertheless, the ordination to an end is of crucial significance to this whole issue. Both the will and the intellect must be developed. As we proceed from an analysis of human actions to an investigation of the habits acquired through the repetition of those actions, we should bear in mind that there are authentic intellectual virtues. We tend to overlook the value they have for our moral life. We are also more familiar with the moral habits, the virtues of the will, than with the virtues of the intellect.

The intellect performs both a theoretical and a practical function. The Greek term *theoria*, as we know, does not refer in this context to theorizing or constructing a scientific system, but to gazing upon or looking at. The theoretical intellect is, therefore, the same as the contemplative intellect. The great 15th-century humanist Ermolao Barbaro, in translating Aristotle from Greek into Latin, rendered the term *theoreticos* as *contemplativus*. The practical intellect, on the other hand, is concerned with our activities, and our activities involve either doing or making. The practical intellect forms judgments concerning our conduct and creativity.

In the theoretical sphere, there are three basic virtues, or intellectual habits. The first and most fundamental is the habit of knowing the first theoretical principles in a certain realm. All of our knowledge is based upon certain initial presuppositions. The first principles in question may be those of a science that encompasses a particular realm of reality or those of wisdom. In either case, they are always the most basic and primary assumptions. Knowledge of these first theoretical principles can later bear fruit and be the foundation for the next virtue, the virtue of science, or lead to the highest intellectual virtue, the virtue of wisdom. We have here, therefore, three intellectual virtues: knowledge of first principles (*intellectus principiorum*), science (*scientia*), and wisdom (*sapientia*).

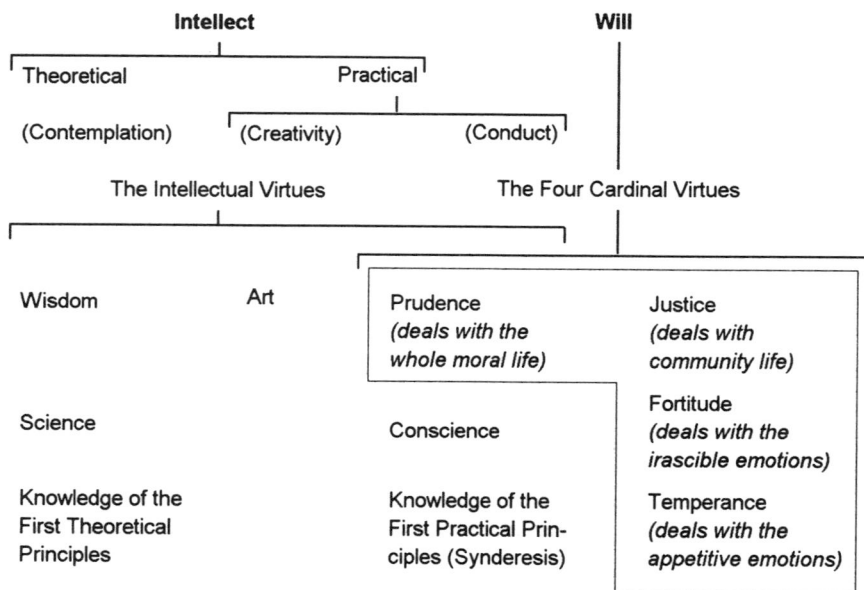

Intellect			**Will**
Theoretical		Practical	
(Contemplation)	(Creativity)	(Conduct)	
The Intellectual Virtues		The Four Cardinal Virtues	
Wisdom	Art	Prudence *(deals with the whole moral life)*	Justice *(deals with community life)*
Science		Conscience	Fortitude *(deals with the irascible emotions)*
Knowledge of the First Theoretical Principles		Knowledge of the First Practical Principles (Synderesis)	Temperance *(deals with the appetitive emotions)*

From a knowledge of first theoretical principles we can derive either a science of particular realms of reality or wisdom, which strives to know reality in terms of its ultimate aspects and causes. Wisdom, the third and highest of the intellectual theoretical virtues, is the art of reflection, an ordination to the whole of reality in the light of its ultimate causes. Philosophy belongs to wisdom, whereas the history of philosophy and all the realms of mathematical, biological, and historical knowledge belong to science.

There are also intellectual virtues that deal with the practical sphere. The virtue of art is related to creativity. This means that when we make something we are truly virtuous if we make it well. A cobbler, a sculptor, a musician, every creator or producer must have the virtue of his or her respective skill or art. With reference to conduct, three intellectual practical virtues are commonly listed. At the basis of these virtues is knowledge of the first principles of conduct, namely, the precepts of the natural law and the content expressed in the Ten Commandments. Knowledge of the first principles of conduct is the virtue of knowing and understanding these most basic presuppositions of human behavior. This virtue has a strange name in Greek: synderesis. St. Thomas says that synderesis is the *habitus continens praecepta legis naturalis* (*ST* I–II, 94, 1, ad 2)—the habit of knowing and applying the precepts of the natural law. The second intellectual virtue in the practical sphere is conscience, which must, through practice, be transformed from a disposition into a habit. Conscience is the habit of applying the general principles of behavior to concrete situations. Conscience, like the other virtues, must be constantly cultivated. Its voice, which expresses what is sometimes called the "subjective norm," is decisive from the moral point of view. Finally, the most important virtue in the practical sphere, and the one analogous to wisdom in the theoretical sphere, is the virtue of prudence, which is the virtue that directs all our actions in all their phases: intention, deliberation, and free choice.

An issue that kept coming up during the discussions at the Second Vatican Council was that Catholics are accustomed to expecting predefined moral solutions and directives in the concrete situations of their daily lives. They wait for guidance from the pastor, directives from the bishop, proclamations from the pope. The Council Fathers said time and again what a misguided approach this was. The Gospel gives us general directives, and the magisterium of the church makes them clearer and more precise, but in every concrete situation each of us is alone in deciding how to apply these general precepts. That is why the virtue of prudence and all the other virtues, especially conscience, are so very important. They are sails we must set at the appropriate moment, opening them to the breeze of the magisterium and the inspiration of the Holy Spirit. Unless these virtues are lived and cultivated, everything will be over-institutionalized and far from an authentically human and Christian life. We should not treat the moral life as though it were a collection of rules, precepts, and principles existing independently of ourselves. The essence of ethical behavior consists in something altogether different. I am not speaking here of situation ethics, where everything changes according to the situation, but of the fact that we must in every situation—and here the advocates of situation ethics are correct—make a new and different decision, because no two concrete situations are ever the same.

The attempt to formulate overly concrete directives is a remnant of casuistry, which gets its name from the Latin term *casus*, meaning a particular moral case that is set up as a model. No moral case, however, is ever repeated. Every situation is different, and we must know how to behave in each new situation. Without an edifice of virtues, we would stand completely helpless before these new situations. We should, therefore, return to emphasizing the virtues throughout the educational process, and we should not think that virtue is an obsolete and useless concept. The development of virtues is necessary for our natural human life.

A very important related issue, and one that St. Thomas also addressed, is the question of whether there is a natural ethics. We must first ask whether, on the purely natural plane, an authentically virtuous life can exist and develop independently of the life of grace and the supernatural virtues, the three divine virtues. St. Thomas says that only the Gospel can show us the proper, final, and deepest end and meaning of morality. The Gospel alone fully reveals the ultimate end. Consequently, the purely natural virtues, if they lack the light of the Gospel and the other aids that flow from the Gospel, will never be fully developed virtues. Nevertheless, St. Thomas says very emphatically that people who live outside the light of the Gospel have genuine, though imperfect, virtue: *Erit quidem vera virtus sed imperfecta* (*ST* II–II, 23, 7)—it will be true virtue, but imperfect.

But why are natural virtues imperfect? Virtues become perfect if a true *connexio virtutum*, a deep and genuine connection, exists among them, and only supernatural love, only charity, can provide this connection. *Simpliciter vera virtus sine caritate esse non potest* (*ST* II–II, 23, 7)— without supernatural love, true virtue in the strict sense cannot exist, because without this love a real *connexio virtutum* cannot arise. And yet we meet true virtue, virtue that is even "heroic" in its own way, in people who live according to the precepts of secular ethics, understood here in the positive and nonideological sense of the term. Virtue cannot, however, be perfect *sine caritate*—without charity. Even today it is possible to speak in a certain sense of secular saints. We all know exceptionally good and noble people, people who seem heroic but who do not have *caritas*. In such cases, we ought not hesitate to acknowledge that we are in the presence of *vera virtus*, true virtue, even if that supernatural connection—of which more will be said later—is lacking.

St. Thomas develops the classical view of the four principal moral virtues: prudence, temperance, fortitude, and justice. These virtues are called "cardinal" (from the Latin word *cardo*, meaning "hinge") because they form the vital hinges, so to speak, that join together the whole structure of our morality. Each of these virtues requires the other three. They all mutually presuppose and complement one another—although their perfect union is brought about only by charity.

Prudence is basically an intellectual virtue, but it deals with our whole moral life. It is essentially, therefore, an intellectual-practical virtue. Prudence is the special art or skill of choosing, in each instance, the means that allow us best to attain our desired end. We are prudent when we habitually understand, foresee, and deliberate. For this to occur, we must train our memory; the memory is an important element in the development of prudence. St. Thomas' analyses are incomparable when, speaking of the virtues and vices in the *Secunda Secundae* of his *Summa*, he describes not only the main virtue itself but the whole train of derivative virtues that accompany it. Following in the train of prudence is a special virtue called docility (*docibilitas*). Docility is the art of making use of the advice of experienced people. This applies primarily to the young, who possess the virtue of docility if they readily avail themselves of the experience of those who have already lived through a great deal. Another virtue that follows in the train of prudence is *eustochia*, the habit of rapidly making right decisions. According to St. Thomas, the greatest obstacles to prudence are lust, which weakens our ability to judge, and prudence of the flesh, which makes us solicitous about the past and future rather than the present. The prudent person should be completely disposed toward the present moment. St. Thomas also mentions other defects that impede the activity of prudence. Prudence, although it is an intellectual virtue, is concerned entirely with our moral life. That is why it is the guiding virtue among the moral virtues.

The next two cardinal virtues are temperance (*temperantia*) and fortitude (*fortitudo*). These two virtues deal with the personal life of individual human beings. They regulate the emotional sphere. Temperance moderates the concupiscible emotions, and fortitude the irascible emotions. The fourth and highest virtue, justice (*iustitia*), deals with community life. It applies to every kind of community, including our community with God, and so it also encompasses the virtue of religion as a natural virtue. The cardinal virtues thus embrace the entire moral life: the realms of the concupiscible emotions, the irascible emotions, and community life. Each of these virtues has its own "terrain," its own particular area of concern.

Temperance is the virtue that teaches us moderation and balance in all areas in which the concupiscible emotions operate. Temperance should not be confused with the virtue of abstinence, which is incidental to temperance and preparatory to the virtue of chastity. Abstinence consists in knowing how to maintain the proper balance between lust and insensibility. We should seek this balance in everything. Excessive abstinence could, for example, lead us to disdain the concupiscible emotions. This would be a vice and not a virtue, because we know that there is nothing wrong with these emotions so long as they are rationally directed to an end. The object of the virtue of temperance is not to eradicate the concupiscible emotions but to employ them and put them to use in the service of attaining a reasonable end. Temperance indirectly concerns the irascible sphere as well, and the derivatives of temperance enumerated by St. Thomas are very beautiful virtues: clemency, humility, and also a virtue that is a favorite in academic circles, *eutrapelia*, which means knowing how to play. Gilson says in one of his works that this topic is connected with the strangest counter-argument in all theology. St. Thomas asks whether feminine coquetry is a sin, and he answers that it cannot be a sin because then those who make fashionable apparel for women would be in a constant state of mortal sin![18]

The virtue of fortitude is not at all the same as daring. Daring is an emotion. One can be very timid and still have a great deal of fortitude. Fortitude controls and tempers the natural reaction of fear, which, like lust, greatly weakens intellectual judgment. Fortitude also curbs all excessive daring. If someone is by nature daring, fortitude will curb the uncontrolled impulses of boldness. Beautiful virtues follow in the train of fortitude, as well. The first is magnanimity, the habit of pursuing noble ends and devoting oneself to great causes. Magnanimity likewise involves respect for great things; a magnanimous person is able to appreciate and admire true greatness. Other virtues connected with fortitude are magnificence, which consists in dealing with great things in a great way, and patience, which involves knowing how to bear afflictions. According to St. Thomas, fortitude is also a powerful school of humility. The antitheses of fortitude are mean spiritedness, vainglory (wanting great things so that we ourselves will look great), and a love of eccentricity and novelty, all of which obstruct humility and diminish magnanimity.

The fourth cardinal virtue is justice (*iustitia*). Justice does not deal with the emotions. Here we leave the terrain of the life of the individual, which is the main concern of temperance and fortitude, and enter the realm of the life of the community. Justice deals with all the different kinds of relationships that exist between human beings and between human beings and spiritual beings—angels and God. There are two kinds of justice, commutative (*commutativa*) and distributive (*distributiva*). If there is a relationship between *A* and *B*, then commutative justice determines what *A* owes *B* and what *B* owes *A*; in other words, it determines what their mutual duties and responsibilities are. If, on the other hand, an individual or a group of individuals is in a position of authority and is responsible for managing the affairs of a society, then the second type of justice, distributive justice, determines how the respective goods will be distributed among the members of that society.

To the sphere of justice also belongs the virtue of religion, which is the expression of justice in our relationship to God. Here we are still far removed from the life of the divine, theological virtues. The virtue of religion speaks only of what we owe to God on the natural plane. The order of grace ushers in an entirely different sense of religion, that reflected in the words of Christ: *No longer will I call you servants, but friends* (John 15:15). Here justice ceases to be the guiding factor, and faith, hope, and charity take over. In the order of grace, we are perfected by faith, hope, and charity.

23

Law and Human Society

From our first conscious moments in childhood to our last conscious moments in life, we must constantly make moral decisions, and conscience is the source and ultimate regulator of these decisions. Conscience needs to be developed. This is an extremely important matter for all morality. Conscience is an intellectual virtue, and so all the principles that apply to the other virtues apply to it as well. We should be continually improving our conscience throughout our life. There is never a point at which we can say that we have a completely perfect, fully mature, properly sensitive conscience. Our conscience should be neither too lax nor too sensitive. It should always abide in the wise mean between laxity and scrupulosity. Here, as with all the other virtues, moderation and balance are best. As we saw earlier, conscience is a habit of the practical intellect, and so it pertains to action, which takes the form of either conduct or creativity. Conscience is a rational habit, and not some sort of gland or muscle! It is the seat of the personal, subjective moral norm. Whatever conscience tells us to do is absolutely obligatory for us.

St. Thomas is very emphatic on this point: we act in a morally good way when we obey the dictates of conscience. This has ramifications for, among other things, the issue of religious conversion. In Thomas' day, there were really no nonbelievers but only different sorts of believers. St. Thomas, therefore, was speaking of the conversion to Christianity of people who held other religious beliefs. His view is unequivocal on this matter. He says that one may not accept Christ if one is not in conscience convinced that it is right to do so. For someone to accept Christianity without being convinced of its truth is a sin.

The basis of the moral life is, according to St. Thomas, the subjective moral norm that resides in our conscience. We act rightly if we abide by this norm and follow it as the voice of truth. But since conscience is a virtue, an intellectual habit, it must also be constantly developed. Throughout our life, however, there is a constant tension between this subjective norm of behavior, which resides in our conscience, and the objective norm, which resides in law. Law expresses an objective norm, one that is independent of our subjective, personal convictions. There will be a tension between these two norms as long as we live, and sometimes we may even be faced with the tragic difficulty of bringing our subjective norm, our conscience, into harmony with the different types of obligatory laws.

Laws are universally binding rules of behavior. They are obligatory, however, only when they are in harmony with the light of the intellect. Laws are not obligatory, says St. Thomas, if they are unreasonable. They are also not obligatory norms if they are contrary to the needs of human nature or fly in the face of objective truth. Laws, as objective rules of behavior, always pertain to communal life. There is no need to stress what a difficult and complicated matter it is to live in community. We are all aware of this since we all live in families of one kind or another. Communal life in a natural family is perhaps even easier than in a family entered into by choice. St. Thomas fully appreciated how difficult it is to live together in a social group. This is also why he says that *omnis lex ad bonum commune ordinatur* (*ST* I–II, 90, 2)—all law is directed toward the common good. Law exists for the sake of promoting the common good, the good of communities of one kind or another. Thomas is speaking here mainly of natural communities, but his words also apply to various kinds of institutional societies.

Only those who govern a community have the right to make and enforce laws for that community. *Nihil aliud est lex quam dictamen practicae rationis in principe, qui gubernat aliquam communitatem perfectam* (*ST* I–II, 91, 1)—law is nothing else than a *dictamen*, a dictate, of practical reason, but the kind of dictate that arises in the mind of one who is the *princeps*, the ruler or leader of a particular community, and also *qui gubernat*, who governs, *aliquam communitatem perfectam*, this in some sense perfect community. St. Thomas is not speaking here of a community that has already attained perfection in the moral sense, but simply of a community that is a true, authentic society—not a community *in fieri*, in the process of becoming, but one already achieved. The Latin term *perfectus*, as we saw earlier, originally meant "achieved," "realized." The sphere of law, because it pertains to society, is intimately connected with the virtue of justice, the virtue that regulates relationships not only between human beings but also between human beings and other rational beings. If we were ever to come in contact with good or bad angels, justice would apply to our relationships to them as well. It also applies to our relationship to God. This is why the virtue of natural religion is closely connected with justice.

In addition to the distinction between commutative and distributive justice mentioned above, St. Thomas also distinguishes between *iustitia humana* and *iustitia legalis*. *Iustitia humana*, human justice, is the justice that regulates the concrete relationships between human beings, both individuals and groups. *Iustitia legalis*, legal justice, is the justice that applies to the functioning of institutions. The transgressions against justice mentioned by St. Thomas are illuminating. They are arranged in a whole galaxy of primary and secondary offenses that destroy the virtue. The greatest vice in relation to any form of justice is what St. Thomas calls "respect of persons," by which he means relating to people on the basis of their status or position rather than on the basis of their personal dignity and worth. This is the most grievous fault, and it gives rise to the most unjust behavior. The Scriptures tell us time and again that God, the most just, without respect of persons, hears the poor, the downtrodden, and those without protection or influence.

In the second place, so to speak, St. Thomas places that which is the direct opposite of justice. Justice consists in giving others their due, and the opposite of this is taking from others what belongs to them. There are various ways of taking away goods that belong to another. Chief among them is taking a life. Herein lies the basis for the prohibition of murder and suicide. Suicide, from this perspective, is a sin against justice. So, too, is taking another's property, every kind of theft and robbery. All such acts violate the natural law.

St. Thomas does not include private property within the natural law itself but lists it among the first consequences of this law. The issue of theft is connected with the concepts of goods and private property. In the case of material goods, St. Thomas adopts a view previously articulated by certain Fathers of the Church, namely, that all are entitled to use the goods of this world. Private property, on the other hand, is a derivative consequence of the natural law. Because the use of goods is a tenet of the natural law itself, and property a consequence of this law, not every instance of taking another's property is theft. This is clearly evident in the well-known principle that the satisfaction of hunger takes precedence over the injunction against the taking of another's property. The example of David eating the sacred bread, to which Jesus refers (see Matt. 12:3–4), is a case in point.

An important area related to justice is professional ethics, which already finds clear expression in St. Thomas' works and continued to develop after his time. The 13th century was a period when cities were blossoming and primitive forms of exchange were giving way to commercial exchange, involving the use of money and capital. Among the issues to which these developments gave rise was the thorny question of usury—lending money for interest. St. Thomas is rather severe when it comes to this practice, but he also understands that, in changing situations, although the moral principle itself must be upheld, the way this principle is applied in professional ethics is subject to change. He also deals with such matters as the conduct of judges, prosecutors, defendants, witnesses, lawyers, merchants, and bankers, who represent the main types of occupations connected in a special way with the whole broadly conceived sphere of activities and obligations pertaining to justice.

In his discussion of taking away goods that belong to another, St. Thomas mentions spiritual goods, which he says are much more important and valuable than material goods. This is why all attacks on spiritual goods, especially on another's good name, are such great offenses. And this applies not only to slander and calumny. From the whole tenor of St. Thomas' remarks, it is clear that he takes very seriously a seemingly less grievous offense, but one that in his eyes is particularly pernicious, namely, ridicule. Ridicule is one of the worst ways of destroying a person's good name.

These are a few of the types of injustice that may arise in relation to the possession of goods, both material and—above all—spiritual. We have been considering them on the purely natural plane. They may perhaps throw a little light on the climate of justice that St. Thomas says must prevail in order for laws to operate justly. We should bear in mind, however, that even if justice reigned supreme, things would still be inadequate and imperfect to the extent that the climate fostered by love is absent. For love, let us recall, is the virtue that joins together the other virtues (*connexio virtutum*) and sublimates their unconditionality. Love also, however, brings us to the order of grace and the realm of the divine virtues.

St. Thomas distinguishes several different types of law based on the different kinds of community: the community of the universe as a whole, the community of humankind, and various smaller human communities. The towering community of the universe is subject to the eternal law (*lex aeterna*), the law established by God to govern all things. Providence is the realization of the eternal law in the progressive history of the world. St. Thomas is far removed from the position of deism, which holds that God set the world in motion, as it were, and then left it on its own. For St. Thomas, God is the first cause of every single event and the designer of the entire plan. God's will permeates absolutely everything down to the smallest detail, and nothing can happen without God's will—not even the activity of free causes that oppose this will. Everything is, in an identical way, willed by God, and this divine eternal law operates continually and in everything.

The natural law (*lex naturalis*) is the eternal law of God applied to the world of human beings. *Lex naturalis nihil aliud est quam participatio legis aeternae in rationali creatura* (*ST* I–II, 91, 2)—the natural law is nothing else than the participation in rational creatures of the eternal law. A little further on St. Thomas writes: *Omnes leges inquantum participent de ratione recta, intantum derivantur a lege aeterna* (*ST* I–II, 93, 3)—all laws, to the extent that they participate in the proper concept of law, are derived from the eternal law of God. Hence, the measure and distinguishing mark of participation in the eternal law (*lex aeterna*) is the reasonableness of a particular law, its agreement with theoretical and practical principles, with right reason. Likewise, in the natural law there are certain presuppositions, tenets, or primary guiding principles (e.g., do good and avoid evil), as well as consequences arising directly from those general principles (e.g., that everyone has a right to own property). We should distinguish between the primary tenets of the natural law and their consequences.

A third kind of law that St. Thomas mentions is human law (*lex humana*). Human laws are positive laws, laws established by human beings. They are meant to regulate and order the different areas of our lives and, so to speak, to fill up the gap that must always exist between the general character of the natural law and the concreteness of the constantly changing situations in which we find ourselves. Human law should attempt to concretize as much as possible all the precepts of the natural law. The positive regulations of human law must be just and reasonable, and we may not obey them if they are contrary to the natural law. This became evident, for example, in the Nuremberg trials, when the charge of genocide was discussed. If certain commands in the realm of human law are in clear conflict with the natural law, then such human law has no authority, and it is even a crime to follow its commands.

The regulation of all social life on earth takes place within the constant tension between our conscience as the subjective norm and law as the objective norm. St. Thomas knows how difficult it is to realize a communal existence in keeping with the proper principles governing it. On this topic, he makes a significant remark: *Optimum speculabile est Deus et optimum agibile vita socialis*—the highest, most perfect object we can know with our theoretical, contemplative intellect is God, and the most excellent work we can perform is social life. Life in the social realm is as sublime and difficult as knowledge of God in the theoretical realm. We are well aware that every society, every community, is a kind of *optimum agibile*—the most excellent work attainable in the sphere of action.

Despite the great difficulty of forming true community, every human being must develop within a society. This even applies to hermits—and if they fail to treat their hermetic life communally, they become outcasts of society and outcasts of the church. If they do not live in intimate union with the supernatural organism of the Mystical Body, they create their own little "shrine," which is a negation of a fully authentic spiritual life.

From a properly developing community, great benefits accrue to the individual. In this regard, St. Thomas writes: *Ille qui quaerit bonum multitudinis ex consequenti etiam quaerit bonum suum, quia bonum proprium non potest esse sine bono communi vel familiae vel civitatis, vel regni (ST* II–II, 47, 10, ad 2)—when we concern ourselves with the common good of society, we thereby also contribute to our own good, since our individual good cannot be realized without the common good of the family, state, or kingdom. St. Thomas here enumerates the main types of human society: family, state, and nation. And although this text refers to the natural order, it can also be applied to the much deeper issue of the mutual bonds between the individual and the church.

24

Community Life

Community life (*vita socialis*; *vita communitatis*), as we have seen, assumes, in the purely natural order, the rank of a very difficult and sublime task, a work demanding the mobilization of all the virtues, especially the virtue of justice. Any community can become a curse. We see this in contemporary life; every type of "human herd" becomes a curse. But a community can also be a blessing. This depends on the development of family virtues, civic virtues, and all the different forms of justice proper to life in society. The concrete models and ideals of social organization change over the course of history. The concrete model of the ideal family changes, and so, too, does the concrete model of the ideal religious community. Their style changes, but their basic principles remain the same. In an era that lends itself to detailed observation, we can see that in our family life (e.g., the way parents relate to children, methods of child-rearing, etc.), even if the same moral principles that guided our grandparents and parents are alive in us and our children, many things have changed considerably.

Changes in religious life were occurring in St. Thomas' day, just as they are in our own. There are different types of communal spirituality and communal life that can be realized in a given epoch. St. Thomas' decision to enter the Dominican Order rather than follow the course of "family politics," which had foreordained him to become a splendid abbot at Monte Cassino, was a revolution in its own way. The Dominicans and Franciscans were a scandal to society; they were looked upon as something on the order of today's hippies. No one wanted to tolerate them. If not for St. Bonaventure, as I mentioned earlier, the whole family of mendicants, including the Franciscans and Dominicans, would have been suppressed at the Council of Lyons in 1274. The secular clergy opposed them. A great campaign was mounted against them; inquiries were sent to bishops, aimed at taking away the charters of the mendicant orders and obliterating the wandering, begging monks. Today in this regard we are also living through an important moment. I believe that, although the Dominicans and Franciscans still contribute a great deal to our age, there appears in every epoch a spirituality that is most suited to the times.

Laski has many ties to the family of the Little Sisters and Little Brothers of Charles de Foucauld. The special charism of this congregation is to witness to a form of contemplation that does not exist independently of the social milieu and that is attained only at the cost of hard labor. This seems to be an extremely important concept for our times. Normal, ordinary paid labor, performed by religious women and men, becomes as though permeated with contemplation. This spirituality does not seek to destroy other spiritualities; it simply introduces a different model, a different style, of spirituality, one that is especially important. Something similar was taking place in the 13th century. We should bear in mind that, in his view of society and ethics, St. Thomas is—contrary to what one sometimes reads—in no way a mouthpiece for an epoch that was on its way out, an epoch of feudal darkness, but is a prophet of a new style of social life that was then just beginning to take shape and that for years thereafter proved extremely viable.

St. Thomas is interested in the organizational model of the city-state. The system of government of such political communities was the subject of numerous studies in the 13th century and was even more vigorously explored in the 15th and 16th centuries. These studies were in large part a theoretical attempt to return to the Greek ideal of a society in which everything can be easily perceived, to a small society where it is easier to form relationships, in contrast to a great empire in which all ties between people tend to disappear. Great debates were waged concerning whether a huge state, such as the Persian or Roman empire, or the Greek city-state is a better form of social organization. St. Thomas is interested in this topic in relation to monastic *communitas*. He makes use of the ancient ideal in order to draft models of various systems in monastic life. To the person in charge he assigns the role of leader, painting a portrait of a perfect prince in keeping with the Dominican spirit. For St. Thomas the leader is not the Benedictine abbot, but one who represents the community. Here we already find a reflection of the democratic notion of electing leaders, which was also a revolutionary innovation, since this practice did not exist in monastic orders. St. Thomas stresses that the leader is *vicem gerens multitudinis* (*ST* I–II, 90, 3), always the exponent of the will of those he or she leads, because the leader is chosen by them. The subjects, in opposing their leader, oppose themselves. St. Thomas regards this fundamental principle as characteristic of the new type of society.

Every leader performs the function of service for the sake of the common good. Consequently, every leader should govern in keeping with the nature of those governed, not crushing them but respecting their freedom. To a large extent, this applies to both political and religious leaders alike. A leader who fails to do this becomes a tyrant. Parents, religious leaders, teachers, political rulers can all become tyrants. With respect to political rulers, a hotly debated issue in the Middle Ages was the question of whether a tyrant may be removed or even killed. It is worth noting here that a group can also function as a first-rate tyrant. When this happens, the group becomes a mob. St. Thomas, employing Aristotelian terminology, uses two terms to designate group tyranny: oligarchy and democracy. An oligarchy is the tyrannical rule of a small group over the masses; a democracy is the tyrannical rule of the people over different classes of society.

St. Thomas, like Aristotle before him, is a pluralist. He says that there can be various types of just systems, not just one. There can be just and good systems when the people rule, and then we have a republic rather than a democracy. When a small group rules in a just way, we then have an aristocracy, because this group is, by assumption, composed of the truly best. Or, finally, we have a monarchy, which is a form of government directed by a single individual, though not necessarily a king. According to St. Thomas, the monarchical system in which one person rules is relatively better than the others because it best safeguards the unity of the community. Moreover, the tyranny of an individual is the least threatening, far less so than the tyranny of a group. Finally, a monarch, if he or she is not a despotic leader, most fully utilizes all the values dispersed throughout the society. This being so, *est... aliquod regimen ex istis commixtum quod est optimum* (*ST* I–II, 95, 4)—the system that is a combination of all the elements of government is the best. In other words, the best system will be the one in which all the values dispersed throughout the society can be put to the best use. St. Thomas calls such a system a *politia bene commixta*—a well-mixed system, a system in which all the values found in a society are utilized and combined.

Who should be the leader, the ruler, the superior? If the aim of society were health or learning, then doctors or scholars should rule, but since the aim of society is the virtuous life of the citizens, the leader should be the one most distinguished in virtue. St. Thomas, therefore, disagrees with Plato's contention that philosophers should rule.

25

The Supernatural Life

We never know who has supernatural life, nor are we able to observe its development. The only experientially perceptible moment—even to the eyes of faith—is the infusion of this life at the moment of baptism. The supernatural life is something entirely different from even the most highly developed virtue of religion. The virtue of religion can be extremely well developed and yet have nothing in common with the supernatural life. This is often the case, for example, in pagans, whose religious life is limited to the natural realm. The supernatural life begins to develop in us—and here St. Thomas is very explicit—at the moment when the theological virtues of faith, hope, and charity begin to dwell in us. "Theological virtues" is not a good name for them. It would be better to call them "divine virtues," since "theological" implies that they are about the *study* of God, whereas "divine" indicates that they are about *God*, that God is their object. When the divine virtues begin to dwell in us and develop in us, the supernatural life begins to germinate and later to blossom. We become a *consors divinae naturae*, a participant of the divine nature. We become a friend of God. Our relationship to God becomes not just one of worship but also one of friendship and unity. This leads us to become like God, something that should already happen embryonically in this life and that will be realized fully in the next.

There is a very profound difference between how the natural virtues operate on the natural plane and how they function once they begin to develop in the climate of the theological virtues. The natural virtues are then raised to a higher level. They are sublimated, transformed, and take on a different nature. They become virtues infused by and subordinated to the life of the three divine virtues, especially the virtue of love. The supernatural life is the double of the natural life. The acquired virtues are transformed into infused virtues. St. Thomas says, as we have seen, that on the level of natural morality there are true virtues but no perfect virtues. The perfection of the virtues is brought about only by the divine virtues, and above all by love. Love causes the virtues that were true but imperfect to become perfect. It also creates a bond among the virtues. The other virtues are linked together by love; they become *virtutes connexae per caritatem*, virtues joined by love. *Caritas* is what unites them. These virtues are no longer disconnected but are harmonized by love, and love cannot exist in this life without faith and hope. St. Paul says that only in the next world will there be no faith or hope—because we will not need them—and love alone will remain (see I Cor. 13:8–13).

Supernatural love allows us to know God and things divine more intimately than and differently from the way in which they are known to a theologian in whom love is absent. Even Satan can know God, and so even Satan can be a theologian without love. But Satan will never be able to know in the way the simplest person knows with love. Love itself is not knowledge, but love endows us with that which causes a *connaturalitas* to arise between us and the object of our knowledge. St. Thomas describes as knowledge *per connaturalitatem* those types of knowledge where we know as though by nature, with ease, things that without *connaturalitas*, without this "affinity of natures," would require very difficult and complicated study. *Compassio, sive connaturalitas ad res divinas fit per caritatem, quae quidem unit nos Deo* (*ST* II–II, 45, 2)—sympathy, or connaturality, in relation to things divine takes place through love, which unites us with God. Not only does *connaturalitas* unite us with God in the realm of love, but it also permits the intellectual virtues to function more effectively in us. Here we see the interdependence of the realms of knowledge and action.

On the natural foundation rest not only the infused and divine virtues, but also the subsequent stages of supernatural life, all of which St. Thomas discusses in detail. These subsequent stages include the Gifts of the Holy Spirit, which in turn prepare the way for life in keeping with the Eight Beatitudes of which the Gospel speaks. The Seven Gifts of the Holy Spirit are, in a sense, the natural and infused virtues with which we are already familiar, only transferred to a higher plane. Here the virtue of wisdom is transformed into the Gift of Wisdom, knowledge of the first theoretical principles into the Gift of Understanding, science into the Gift of Knowledge, prudence into the Gift of Counsel, and fortitude into the Gift of Fortitude. Justice in the temporal order embraces the virtue of religion, which is subsequently united with the Gift of Piety. To justice and temperance correspond the Gift of the Holy Spirit known as Fear of the Lord. Thus, the natural virtues, which at a lower stage become the infused virtues, prepare the ground for the Gifts of the Holy Spirit. The Eight Beatitudes, in turn, are the pinnacle of the whole supernatural life. They form the last and highest stage of the life of grace, which prepares us to receive the *lumen gloriae*, the light of glory, which will bring about the fulfillment of both the cognitive and the appetitive order in us. In the beatific vision that will take place as a result of the light of glory, as well as in every human act, knowledge and love will be most intimately united.

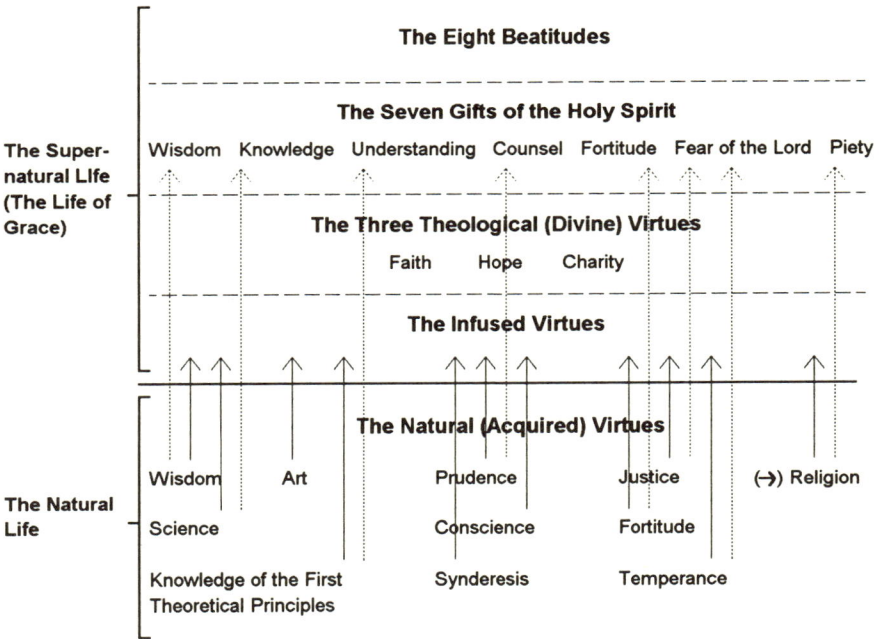

The Eight Beatitudes

The Seven Gifts of the Holy Spirit

The Supernatural Life (The Life of Grace)

| Wisdom | Knowledge | Understanding | Counsel | Fortitude | Fear of the Lord | Piety |

The Three Theological (Divine) Virtues

Faith   Hope   Charity

The Infused Virtues

The Natural (Acquired) Virtues

The Natural Life

Wisdom   Art   Prudence   Justice   (→) Religion

Science   Conscience   Fortitude

Knowledge of the First Theoretical Principles   Synderesis   Temperance

Notes

1. Stefan Swiezawski, "O roli filozofii i o niektorych jej typach" ("On the Role of Philosophy and Some of Its Types"), *Rozum i tajemnica* (*Reason and Mystery*) by Swiezawski (Krakow: ZNAK, 1960) 103–104.

2. See René Voillaume, *Au Coeur des Masses: La vie religieuse des Petits Frères du Père de Foucauld* (Paris: Éditions du Cerf, 1957).

3. Stefan Swiezawski, "Quelques déformations de la pensée de St. Thomas dans la tradition thomiste," *Aquinas and Problems of His Time*, Mediaevalia Lovaniensia, Series 1, Studia 5, ed. G. Verbeke and D. Verhelst (Leuven: Leuven UP, 1976) 38–54.

4. See A. C. Rzewuski, *A travers l'invinsible cristal* (Paris: Plon, 1976).

5. Alexander Fedorowicz, "Kardynal Journet" ("Cardinal Journet"), *Tygodnik Powszechny* 17 (1965), rpt. in *W nurcie zagadnien posoborowych*, vol. 7 (Warszawa: Wydaw. Siostr Loretanek-Benedyktynek, 1975) 325–329.

6. Ernest Friche, *Études Claudelinnes* (Porrentruy: Éditions des Portes de France, 1943).

7. Jacques Maritain, *Distinguish to Unite, or The Degrees of Knowledge*, trans. Gerald B. Phelan (New York: Scribner, 1959).

8. To anyone interested in reading a beautiful discourse on the poverty and splendor of metaphysics, I recommend the chapter entitled "The Grandeur and Poverty of Metaphysics" in Maritain's *Distinguish to Unite*.

9. On the existence of evil, see J. M. Garrigues, *Dieu sans idee du mal* (Paris, 1982). This excellent book is actually a commentary on St. Thomas' words: *Malum non habet in Deo ideam* (*ST* I, 15, 3, ad 1)—God has no concept of evil.

10. Étienne Gilson, *Le Thomisme* (Paris: Vrin, 1944) 259.

11. G. K. Chesterton, *St. Thomas Aquinas* (New York: Image, 1959).

12. See Stefan Swiezawski, "Centralne zagadnienie tomistycznej nauki o duszy (*Commensuratio animae ad hoc corpus*)" ["The Central Issue of the Thomistic Doctrine on the Soul (*Commensuratio animae ad hoc corpus*)"], *Przeglad Filozoficzny* 44 (1948): 131–191.

13. See Leszek Kuc, "Z badan nad pojeciem 'theoria' w szkole tomistycznej XV wieku" ("A Study of the Concept of *Theoria* in 15th-Century Thomism"), *Studia z dziejow mysli sw. Tomasza z Akwinu*, ed. S. Swiezawski and J. Czerkawski (Lublin: Tow. Naukowe KUL, 1978) 47–90.

14. See Goethe, *Faust*, Part I, 1, 2.

15. "Spinoza ne commence ni par les choses ni par le moi, mais par Dieu" (S. Zac, "Spinoza," *Histoire de la philosophie*, vol. 2 [Paris 1973] 458, qtd. in *Encyclopédie de la Pléiade* 36).

16. J. Domenski, in his book *Erazm i filozofia* [*Erasmus and Philosophy* (Wroclaw 1973) 36], speaks of Erasmus' *Convivium Religiosum* as being "noted for its avowal of Socrates' holiness."

17. *"Radix libertatis est voluntas sicut subjectum; sed sicut causa est ratio"* (*ST* I–II, 17, 1, ad 2).

18. *ST* II–II, 169, 2. See Étienne Gilson, *Tomizm* [*Thomism*], trans. J. Rybalt (Warsaw 1960) 416.

Index of Names